THE OTHER AMERICA

THE OTHER AMERICA
THE AFRICAN AMERICAN
EXPERIENCE

ROBERT L. WALSH, M.Ed.

AND

LEON F. BURRELL, Ph.D., MSW

Cover and text design: Barbara Jones

Cover image: Courtesy of Documentary Photo Aids, Inc., Lake Mary, FL

Printed by: Techniprint, Inc., Lebanon, NH

First edition

Library of Congress Control Number: 2001094550

ISBN 1-930149-05-0

published by

Booksurge, LLC
5341 Dorchester Rd. Suite 16,
N. Charleston, SC 29418

Dedicated to

The Tuskegee Airmen
and
The Montford Point Marines

TABLE OF CONTENTS

ACKNOWLEDGMENTS

We are grateful for the encouragement and support we received as we wrote *The Other America*. From the beginning our colleagues, friends, students, and members of the community confirmed the need for this book. As we progressed we asked professional educators and members of the public to review and critique our work. The comments we received were surprising only in the intensity of the reviewers' thirst for more information about the African American experience. We thank the following individuals for reviewing our work:

Mr. Steven Davis, Head of the Upper School, Webb School, Knoxville, TN;

Dr. Charles E. Memusi Johnson, Vermont Advisory Committee to the United States Commission on Civil Rights, and Safe Schools Coordinator, Vermont, Department of Education, Thetford, VT;

Mr. Maurice Mahoney, Social Studies Department, South Burlington High School, South Burlington, VT;

Mr. Roy Morrison, Writers' Publishing Cooperative, Warner, NH;

Mr. Allen Shapiro, Social Studies Department, Swampscott High School, Swampscott, MA;

Mrs. Sylvia Jarvis Smith, columnist, South Burlington, VT.

Sheila Mable, Chair of the English Department of South Burlington High School, South Burlington, Vermont, Marigrace Engel of South Burlington, Vermont, and Mr. Rob Schumann of Woodstock, Vermont edited our work. They challenged us with their constructive comments and attention to detail. We appreciate their professional efforts on our behalf.

Ms. Barbara Jones of Lebanon, NH, provided invaluable assistance composing the copy, coordinating the pictures, and designing the cover. She became a valued advisor and enthusiastic supporter of our work. She also became a friend.

We are particularly grateful to Mr. Herbert Fabricand of Documentary Photo Aids Inc., Lake Mary, Florida for donating the pictures that appear in *The Other America*. The pictures tell their own powerful story.

We wish to express our appreciation to the following individuals and for their advice, counsel and support:

The Honorable Philip Hoff, Vermont Advisory Committee to the United States Commission on Civil Rights, and former Governor of the State of Vermont;

Mrs. Claire Buckley, Librarian, Community Library South Burlington, Vermont;

The Honorable Francis Brooks, Vermont House of Representatives;

Dr. Marc Hull, former Commissioner of Education, State of Vermont;

Mr. Stephan Morse, Executive Director of The Windham Foundation;

Mr. Marc Pentino, U.S. Commission on Civil Rights, Washington, D.C.; and,

The Honorable Douglas Racine, Lieutenant Governor, State of Vermont.

We are especially indebted to Sandy Walsh and Toni Trombley for their love, support and encouragement.

INTRODUCTION

The Other America provides insight into the origins of the complex racial problems facing America. It discusses the pragmatic economic reasons for slavery in Colonial America and in the United States. The book examines how the legacy of the slave system was perpetuated during the years of Jim Crow. And how the accomplishments of the Civil Rights Movement have mitigated, but have not eliminated, prejudice and racial discrimination in American culture. It concludes with an overview of the events, following the assassination of Dr. Martin Luther King, Jr., that have shaped the African American experience as the twentieth century came to a close.

The Other America introduces the reader to African American men and women who have shaped history such as Benjamin Bannecker, Marcus Garvey, Paul Robeson, Adam Clayton Powell, Althea Gibson, James Forten, Richard Allen, and Phillis Wheatley. It provides new insights about prominent personalities such as Jackie Robinson, Joe Louis, Malcolm X, and Dr. King.

While reading *The Other America*, the reader is encouraged to challenge the racial prejudices, stereotypes and myths that are so prevalent in the United States today.

1

Ancient Africa: A Rich History

In the 1970s, White Americans were startled by the sudden appearance of colorful African garments and unusual bushy hairstyles called Afros among Black Americans. Conking, the painful burning process of straightening the natural curly hair of the American Negro to create a White appearance was no longer in vogue. Neither was the traditional greasy slicked back look. The *zoot suits* of the 1940s had been replaced by more traditional garb in the fifties and sixties. But now in the seventies, men were wearing full-length robes and shirts with billowing sleeves while women wore colorful saris and turbans. Both sexes were adorned with bracelets and jewelry. Even the language seemed to change as Blacks greeted one another with hand signs and the salutation of *brother* or *sister*.

White Americans were confused by the new assertiveness of their Black brethren and the public calls for Black Power and Black Pride. However, had Whites been previously taught something other than an Euro-centric view of world history, they would have understood that the Black community was awakening to its rich heritage, a heritage that had been suppressed in the United States for almost 300 years.

The roots of Black America are not found in the cotton fields of the mythical plantation Tara. Black Americans are the direct descendants of rich societies in Western Africa: the ancient kingdoms of Ghana, Songhay, and Mali. They are also the descendants of a culture that was influenced by the Greeks, Romans, Ethiopians, Egyptians, and others. However, until the onset of the Civil Rights movement in the late 1950s, there was little understanding or appreciation in the United States of the heritage of Black Americans.

For many Americans their first true exposure to the history of Black America came in the form of the 1975 television production of Alex Haley's magnificent book *Roots.* Prior to that Americans, Black and White, had little exposure to African history in their schooling. When mentioned at all, Africa was generally portrayed as the Dark Continent. It was a place where fierce tribes of Black people ran around naked carrying spears. Cannibalism was a daily practice, and White people who ventured there could expect to end up in a boiling pot as the main meal for the local chieftain. Over time these misconceptions of Africa were perpetuated in America's view of its Black citizens. The misconceptions had also been reinforced by over 200 years of slavery and degradation.

An understanding of the institution of slavery is fundamental to any study of African American history. Most Black Americans can trace their ancestry to the shores of Western Africa. It was there that modern slavery began in the 17th century when Portuguese explorers brought home their first captives for sale in European markets.

Slavery existed in Africa for hundreds of years before the Portuguese began exporting slaves to Europe. However, there is a considerable difference between the slavery practiced in ancient times and that of modern slavery. Ancient slavery, generally, was the result of war. The conquered became the slaves of the conquerors. There was little stigma attached to being a slave and often slaves were accepted and admired members of the community. Certainly there were abuses, but in general it was understood by slave and master alike that their roles could just as easily reverse should war occur. Modern slavery was based on economics. The bottom line of profit and loss changed the nature of slavery and from it evolved the concept of racial inferiority and the acceptance of human beings as chattel.

❝

Western Africa is approximately half the size of the United States. Its geography is a mixture of rain forests and grasslands called savannas. To the north is the Sahara Desert. Despite the imposing obstacle of the desert, the people of Western Africa had for centuries traded with the Arabs of Northern Africa exchanging gold and cloth for much needed salt. It was from these northern Arabs that the region acquired its name, the Sudan. Sudan in Arabic means the *land of the Blacks.*

From 700 to 1000 the kingdom of Ghana was at the height of its power in western Sudan. Ghana means warrior king and was used as a preface to the King's name. As such the land became colloquially known as Ghana. The actual name of the kingdom was Kumbi. Foreigners also knew it simply as the *land of the gold.*

Ghana's wealth came from gold. Although the land had no gold fields of its own, Ghana's geographical location allowed it to control trade. Arabs bringing salt from the north had to cross Ghana to reach the gold from the region of the Senegal River. Ghana acted as the middleman providing not only a marketplace, but also the resources of its 200,000-man army as protection.

In addition to its wealth Ghana's strength was derived from several other factors. Its large army, as a result of Ghana's superior technology, was equipped with iron spears. Ghana also had excellent government organization and leadership. It had developed an efficient system of taxation and welcomed traders. At the invitation of the King, Muslim traders settled and established a trading center approximately six miles from the capital city of Kumbi. The Muslim settlers also brought their Islamic religion to the region. The King and his followers, however, remained true to their African beliefs.[1]

3

At its apex ancient Ghana exhibited all the attributes of a complex modern day society: an effective system of government supported by a strong army, a stable economy based on trade, and a foreign policy that focused on cooperation to ensure peace. Women by tradition held high places in government, and there was a strong sense of family and clan that united the people. The King was considered God's representative and thus the religious as well as the secular leader. If there was a weakness in the structure of this society, it was that the people identified too closely with the personage of the King as opposed to the concept of a state. Thus in 1076 when Muslim warriors attacked and captured the capital city of Kumbi, Ghana suffered a blow from which it never recovered.[2]

In the years following the disintegration of Ghana, a new empire, Mali, stepped forward to fill the void. Mali existed as early as the year 1000, but its rise to greatness coincided with the reign of Sundiata Keita, its ruler from 1230-1255. He captured the gold fields of his neighbors to the south and expanded the empire north to include portions of the Sahara and east to the Senegal River.

Sixty years after Sundiata's rule, a new emperor or Mansa ascended to the throne. Mansa Musa, the grandnephew of Sundiata, ruled from 1312 until his death in 1337. During his reign Mali reached the height of its power. Mali flourished as a center not only for trade, but for scholarship as well. The city of Timbuktu was renowned for its university and at one point it was said that books were the city's most profitable item of trade.

After the death of Mansa Musa, Mali suffered a period of decline. There were rebellions by states within the empire. One of those states, Songhay, was led by a powerful King called Sunni Ali. Sunni Ali captured the city of Timbuktu in 1468 and captured most of the Niger River valley, establishing the empire of Songhay. He was succeeded by Askia Mohammed, who extended the empire until it covered an area about the size of Western Europe. In 1590 Moroccan raiders armed with guns attacked Songhay, and the age of the great empires of the

Western Sudan came to an end. However, the empires of Ghana, Mali, and Songhai represent an age of enlightenment predating the European Renaissance. From these empires came sophisticated systems of government and social, economic, and religious practices that continue in the 21st century.

☾

The geography of the Western Sudan, the body's need for salt, and the human desire for gold created conditions for trading among the peoples of the region. In turn, the desire to trade influenced the development of the culture. Trading demanded the establishment of rules and procedures. In Ghana traders never came face to face. They practiced "dumb barter" or silent trading. Arabs arriving in Ghana would place their piles of salt in the marketplace and then leave. Next, their opposite numbers would enter the market place and put an amount of gold next to a pile of salt. Then they too would leave, signaling their departure by beating a drum. On hearing the drum, the Arabs would return and evaluate the amount of gold they had received. If satisfied, they would take the gold and head for home. If they were not satisfied, the process would be repeated until agreement was reached.[3] In the United States today many fund-raising organizations employ the tactic of the silent auction.

Trading also required that people be able to understand one another. Therefore, it was necessary to learn a common language, which in turn facilitated the development of communication and literacy skills among the peoples of the Africa. In the Western Sudan the Mandinka language became the predominant trading language. In Central Africa the Hausa language dominated. Swahili was the language of the eastern coast. Today Swahili is spoken by more than 30 million Africans.

Both trade and military conquest brought the Islamic religion to the kingdoms of Western Sudan. At first, as previously noted in the discussion of Ghana's capital city Kumbi, the Kings were careful to keep the religion of the Islamic traders separate from the traditional African religious beliefs. The capital was actually two cities separated by approximately six miles. In the business district the Islamic religion was practiced. In the adjacent city, which was occupied by the King, traditional religious practices were followed and Islam was banned. Eventually, Islam gained a strong place in African culture.

Mansa Musa was a devout Muslim who faithfully practiced the Five Pillars of Islam. One of those pillars requires Muslims, who are physically and financially capable of doing so, to make at least one pilgrimage to the holy city of Mecca. Mansa Musa made his pilgrimage in 1324. He took with him some 60,000 people and more than a ton of gold. As he traveled to Mecca, he distributed gold so freely that he actually caused its devaluation.

❨

In Central Africa Christianity was deeply rooted in the kingdom of Ethiopia. This remarkable kingdom was initially an ancient city-state called Aksum. Aksum was to Africa what the cities of Rome and Sparta were to the Mediterranean. Ethiopia, then, was a world power long before the birth of Christ or the development of European societies. Its Emperor traces his lineage back to the Queen of Sheba. In approximately 330 AD the city-state of Aksum accepted Christianity as its national religion. Ethiopia remains Christian today and has claim to being the longest continuous Christian Empire.

Christian and Islamic beliefs, the importance of family and community, music and the arts, military and athletic achievement, successful economic and political enterprise are all characteristics of modern day Black America. The roots of these characteristics are found in its African heritage. For more than two centuries many of these characteristics, abilities and beliefs were suppressed first in slavery and then by *Jim Crow* segregation laws. Hopefully we have reached a point where they can now flourish in America.

The heritage of Black America emanates from the radiant societies of ancient Africa. Far from being the Dark Continent, Africa was a center of trade and intellectual accomplishment at a time when the societies of Europe were merely emerging. Ironically, the cloak of darkness that descended on Africa was white. King Henry the Navigator of Portugal sent his ships along the western shores of Africa in search of riches. They found an invaluable product, cheap labor in the form of human slaves. For the next 400 years Europeans drained Africa of millions of its best and brightest people. Later they divided the continent into colonies, drained it of its economic resources, and attempted to obliterate its culture.

The traditions and culture of ancient Africa crossed the Atlantic in the minds and souls of the slaves destined for America. Despite staggering obstacles, they have survived and have become an integral part of American culture.

NOTES

1. Leon E. Clark, ed., *The African Past and the Coming of the European* (New York: Praeger Publishers 1970), p.17
2. *The Search for Black Identity: Proud Heritage from Africa (Part 1):* Pleasantville, New York: Guidance Associates Sound Filmstrips, 1970
3. Leon E. Clark, ed., pp.13-14

2

Colonial Black America: Abolitionist Stirrings

When the average American thinks of slavery, images of the movie *Gone With the Wind* appear. Tara, the imposing plantation house, dominates the countryside. Scarlett O'Hara, beautifully coiffured and in her finest satin dress, is being attended to by her faithful, graying servant. In the fields slaves sing spirituals while they pick the cotton. Slavery had many faces, but the one we most commonly accept is generally false.

Slavery was not something new or unique to North America. It had been in existence for centuries and had taken different forms. Ancient slavery, in the days of the Egyptian Pharaohs, was in great part the result of war. When armies met on the battlefield, the losers became the slaves of the victors. Although ancient slavery was indeed harsh, it was ameliorated in that the slave owners knew they too could become slaves if their country's fortunes changed for the worse. Modern slavery, dating from the Period of Exploration, was based on economics.

As the Europeans explored the coast of Africa, they exported slaves to work in bondage in Europe. England and Portugal, two countries that employed slaves, provide early insight into future attitudes toward slaves in the Americas. Slaves arriving in England were not assimilated into society and today England remains predominantly White Anglo-Saxon. On the other hand, the physical characteristics and complexion of the Portuguese are a clear reminder of how the African slaves were integrated into that culture.

The purpose of exploring the New World was clearly for economic gain. As the Spanish colonized South America, Mexico, and the West Indies, they quickly realized that the climate and terrain were suitable for the cultivation of sugar and other products for export. They cultivated large blocks of land, employing farming techniques that had been successful in Africa. Those techniques, however, required the use of a large, cheap labor force. With plenty of Indians available, the Spanish first attempted to hire them and later tried to enslave them. Neither proved successful. Indians proved to be poor workers. One of the primary reasons for their inability to work was that they succumbed to new diseases that the Spanish brought from Europe and from which the Indians were not immune. To rectify this problem, Bartolome De Las Casas, a Catholic Bishop and former Conquistador, recommended the importation of African slaves to provide the labor force. The Africans had extensive contact with Europeans and were immune to their diseases. Thus African slavery was established in the Americas long before the first cotton field was planted in what would become the American Colonies.

Africans first arrived in North America at Jamestown, Virginia in August, 1619. We know they came by ship, but why they came is uncertain. Shortly thereafter the first African baby was born in America. His father was a man named Antony. His mother was a woman called Isabella. They named their child William and the history of Black America began.[4]

During the first 40 or so years that Africans were in America, they were absorbed into a society that was divided along economic rather than racial lines. Most Blacks during this period were indentured servants. Blacks and Whites worked side-by-side in the same jobs. They socialized together. They sang and danced. They shared common hardships and joys. They fell in love. Intermingling of the races was not uncommon. Surprisingly, some Blacks who were economically well off even owned slaves of their own.[5]

The development of sugar, tobacco, and cotton as major export items required large labor forces to work the plantations. The Spanish had found Indians to be unreliable. In addition to getting sick, the Indians often would run away and rejoin their tribes or simply hide in the familiar terrain. White workers proved to be equally unsatisfactory. Most poor Whites came to the New World as indentured servants. Once their obligation terminated, they were free to go. Many didn't wait for their obligation to expire and simply left. Being White, they could blend in with the rest of society and were difficult to catch. They were also protected from enslavement by the laws of their mother country. Africans, on the other hand, were the perfect answer to the problem. They were strong and good workers. They did not get sick. Being Black, they did not blend in and were easy to identify. They were not protected by law, and once in America they were 3,000 miles from home with nowhere to go. Finally, there was a plentiful supply in Africa, and there were African slave merchants, known as Slatees, who were willing to sell their brethren to the highest bidder. Thus, African slaves provided a stable labor force that was cheap to obtain and did not have to be paid.

As the Colonial economy became increasingly reliant on the production of cotton, tobacco, and sugar, the requirement for slave labor increased. By the 1660s, Maryland and Virginia had passed laws making Blacks slaves for life and prohibiting inter-racial marriage. These laws stayed on the books in many American states well into the 1960s, and shaped American attitudes toward interracial dating and sexual conduct that are still prevalent in the year 2000.

The passage of laws making Blacks slaves for life and banning inter-racial marriage were direct steps in creating and controlling the needed labor force. From the outset, it was recognized that maintaining an economy based on slave labor required one race to be superior and the other inferior. This was accomplished by separating the races. It was important that the inferior race never see any of the frailties or natural defects of the superior race. It was equally important that the superior race did not form emotional attachments or bond with the inferior race.

It was assumed that as time passed, residual attachments between the races would fade as the elders died off. Newborns of both races would then be raised within the system and would know no better. Once this happened, the culture of slavery was established and became increasingly difficult to dislodge. Slavery in North America lasted for over 240 years. Black Americans never accepted the concept and resisted actively and passively.

Once established, slavery ensured the success of the cotton, tobacco, and sugar economies. These products then spawned other business that also relied on slave labor. In New England a booming ship building business emerged providing the means of transportation for the cotton, sugar, and tobacco. New England also provided the ships to support a new business, the transportation of human cargo from Africa to the Americas. Thus, in the northern colonies slavery was accepted as well. However, unlike the plantation slaves of the South, many of the slaves in the North worked as artisans or laborers in a variety of fields. The end result was that the economy of the American Colonies and subsequently that of the United States became absolutely dependent on slave labor. As we shall see, the abolition of slavery in the years to come was not something to be taken lightly and would be no easy task.

❨

Today we view slavery with repugnance. Surely the thoughtful people of Colonial times must have struggled with the idea of trading in human beings. How then did they justify such actions? Ironically, religion proved to be the salve that soothed their consciences. Whites justified abducting Africans as slaves by reasoning that the Africans were not Christians and therefore it was permissible. There was plenty of precedent for this line of reasoning. In the 1500s, the Spanish had used much the same rationale when enslaving the Indians. Once enslaved, Africans arriving in Colonial America were baptized as Christians. They were then told that their present condition of slavery was their hell on earth and that, if they performed their duties faithfully, they would reap their reward in heaven. Selective use of the Bible proved an effective method of controlling slaves for many years.

Slaves landing in the Catholic colonies of the West Indies and South America were generally treated better. They were allowed to retain many of their customs and interracial mixing was accepted. A close look at the physical characteristics and coloring of our present day Latin American neighbors confirms this.

In the English colonies of North America, it was a different story entirely. Slaves unfortunate enough to land in the English colonies were systematically denied their African culture: their religion, their customs, their music, and their language. Slaves were subjected to a "breaking in" period. This period lasted about three years. During this time a new slave was placed under the supervision of a veteran slave who in turn taught the newcomer the intricacies of slaving. The new slave was taught to speak broken English, given a new name, disciplined, and taught the skills needed to be a productive member of the work force. He was not taught to read. Any resistance or slacking on the part of the new slave resulted in his supervisor being punished.

❰

The slave trade in America lasted approximately 240 years. It could have ended sooner, but in the politics of the day, the framers of the U.S. Constitution acquiesced to the demands of their southern colleagues and protected the institution of slavery by including Article IV, Section 2 in that document. However, the Rights of Man Movement and the principles of the American Revolution played a significant part in stopping the importation of slaves at the beginning of the 19th century. Nevertheless, by the time the opening shots of the Civil War landed on the parapets of Fort Sumter, there were some four million Black slaves in the United States.

Where did they come from? Most came from the West Coast of Africa, from the area that had once been the ancient kingdoms of Ghana, Songhay, and Mali. They came from many different tribes and many different personal situations. There were princes and paupers. It made no difference. A man could step outside his hut for a final breath of fresh air before going to sleep and awaken in the foul smelling hold of a slave ship on route to the Americas.

The slave trade was a brutal trade. Newly captured slaves were assembled at staging areas, usually forts, near the African seacoast. There they were branded like cattle and herded aboard the slave ships for the three-month passage to the Americas. Conditions on the ships were filthy. Slaves were forced to lie side-by-side, chained together, below decks. The air was foul with the stench of human excrement and the smell of death from those who passed away the previous night. Each day the slaves were brought above deck and forced to exercise. Those who balked or refused were whipped. Some slaves broke free and jumped overboard only to be met by the ever-present school of sharks that followed the ships. Others tried various means of resistance. Some refused to eat and had their teeth bashed out for their trouble. Other resisters were simply killed on the spot.

Bad as conditions were on these ships, it was still very important to the Captain that his cargo arrived at its destination safely and in good health. After all, this was a business and his profit margin depended on delivering serviceable goods. On arrival in America, the slaves were again herded into staging areas where they remained while they recovered from the ravages of the voyage. During this time they were fattened up and reconditioned for the auction to come. The concern was to have the product look its best in order to bring top dollar.

The slave auction was not much different than auctions of today: the

Drawing of a typical ship used to transport slaves from Africa across the Atlantic Ocean to the Americas. *Image courtesy of Documentary Photo Aids.*

auction was advertised, people bid on products, people made deals, business was conducted, and people socialized. Unlike today, at the slave auction people sold people. Human beings were placed on the block and exhibited for sale. Some were stark naked to ensure that the buyer had a good idea of what was being purchased. The price varied according to age, sex and physical condition. Men were sold away from their wives. Children were sold away from their mothers. Families were destroyed. It made no difference. What mattered were the needs of the customers. Once the auction was over, the owners returned to their plantations with the newly purchased chattel, and the ships sailed east to start the cycle once again.

When the slave trade was abolished, the planters devised a new method of replenishing their stocks. They grew them. Selective male slaves were forced to be *studs.* Women were forced to bear children and

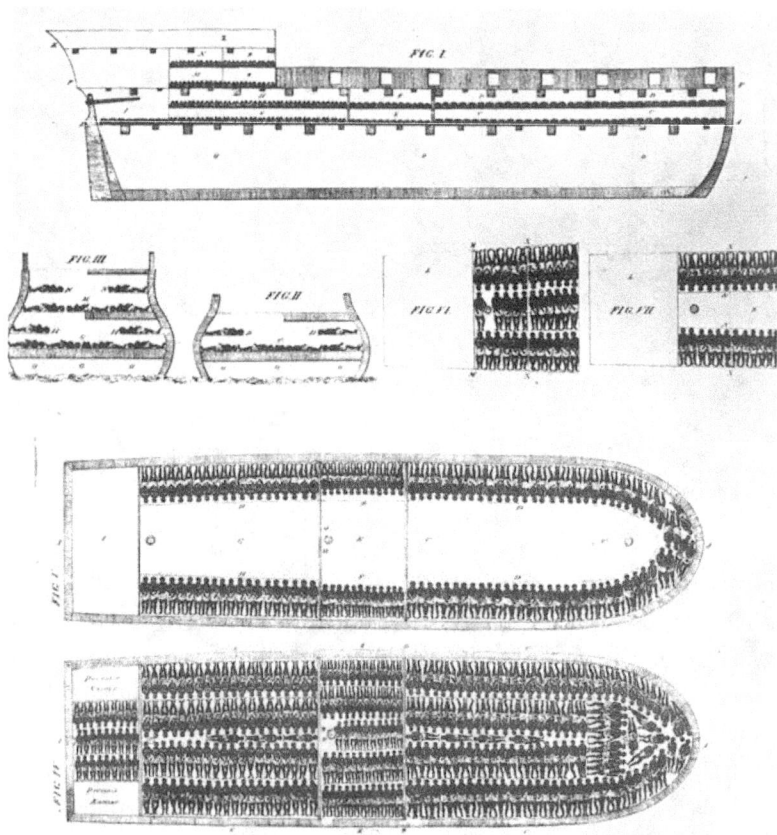

Loading plan for the slave ship Brookes. The Brookes was only 100 feet long and 25 feet wide, but it carried as many as 609 slaves. The average space allowed each person was about sixteen inches wide and five and a half feet long. *Image courtesy of Documentary Photo Aids.*

Price, Birch, & Company was a successful slave-trading firm located in Alexandria, Virginia. The company kept newly arrived slaves in this building until they were sold. The picture was taken around 1864. *Image courtesy Documentary Photo Aids.*

became known as *breeding machines*. The slave trade was indeed a brutal trade. It decimated the finest of African society and left a legacy of racism, distrust, and economic and social problems that still plague us today throughout America.

❮

While Black America toiled in chains, White America chafed at the oppression of King George III of England. While Blacks picked cotton, Whites gathered at the local pub and complained about the politics of the day. Economics was the driving force as White America rebelled at the prospect of increased taxation from the mother country. The resulting revolution split the colonies from England and gave birth to the United States of America.

The American Revolution produced heroes for the ages and a con-

BY

HEWLETT & BRIGHT.

SALE OF

VALUABLE SLAVES,

(On account of departure)

The Owner of the following named and valuable Slaves, being on the eve of departure for Europe, will cause the same to be offered for sale, at the NEW EXCHANGE, corner of St. Louis and Chartres streets, on *Saturday,* May 16, at Twelve o'Clock, *viz.*

1. SARAH, a mulatress, aged 45 years, a good cook and accustomed to house work in general, is an excellent and faithful nurse for sick persons, and in every respect a first rate character.

2. DENNIS, her son, a mulatto, aged 24 years, a first rate cook and steward for a vessel, having been in that capacity for many years on board one of the Mobile packets; is strictly honest, temperate, and a first rate subject.

3. CHOLE, a mulatress, aged 36 years, she is, without exception, one of the most competent servants in the country, a first rate washer and ironer, does up lace, a good cook, and for a bachelor who wishes a house-keeper she would be invaluable; she is also a good ladies' maid, having travelled to the North in that capacity.

4. FANNY, her daughter, a mulatress, aged 16 years, speaks French and English, is a superior hair-dresser, (pupil of Guillac,) a good seamstress and ladies' maid, is smart, intelligent, and a first rate character.

5. DANDRIDGE, a mulatoo, aged 26 years, a first rate dining-room servant, a good painter and rough carpenter, and has but few equals for honesty and sobriety.

6. NANCY, his wife, aged about 24 years, a confidential house servant, good seamstress, mantuamaker and tailoress, a good cook, washer and ironer, etc.

7. MARY ANN, her child, a creole, aged 7 years, speaks French and English, is smart, active and intelligent.

8. FANNY or FRANCES, a mulatress, aged 22 years, is a first rate washer and ironer, good cook and house servant, and has an excellent character.

9. EMMA, an orphan, aged 10 or 11 years, speaks French and English, has been in the country 7 years, has been accustomed to waiting on table, sewing etc.; is intelligent and active.

10. FRANK, a mulatto, aged about 32 years speaks French and English, is a first rate hostler and coachman, understands perfectly well the management of horses, and is, in every respect, a first rate character, with the exception that he will occasionally drink, though not an habitual drunkard.

All the above named Slaves are acclimated and excellent subjects; they were purchased by their present vendor many years ago, and will, therefore, be severally warranted against all vices and maladies prescribed by law, save and except FRANK, who is fully guaranteed in every other respect but the one above mentioned.

TERMS:—One-half Cash, and the other half in notes at Six months, drawn and endorsed to the satisfaction of the Vendor, with special mortgage on the Slaves until final payment. The Acts of Sale to be passed before WILLIAM BOSWELL, Notary Public, at the expense of the Purchaser.

New-Orleans, May 13, 1835.

27

The sale of slaves was routinely advertised in American newspapers. *Image courtesy of Documentary Photo Aids.*

cept of government unparalleled in the history of human endeavor. Among the better known heroes are George Washington, Nathan Hale, Thomas Jefferson, John and Samuel Adams, Patrick Henry, and of course Barbara Frietchie. Every American school child can relate the exploits of Paul Revere and tell you that one lantern in the belfry of the Old North Church meant the British would be advancing by land. But there were other heroes as well. They just aren't as well known.

Crispus Attucks was a former slave. A seaman of middle age and imposing presence, he was a familiar figure around the Boston docks. On the night of March 4, 1770, Attucks was among a group of Bostonians arguing with some English sentries. As the confrontation became more heated, the English called for reinforcements. During the scuffle a shot was fired. Crispus Attucks fell dead. The first casualty of the American Revolution was Black.[6] It is an irony that has gone unnoticed in many accounts of American History but is not lost on the Black community.

While Crispus Attucks was a civilian, Black soldiers also distinguished themselves during the Revolution. At Lexington there were Black Minutemen: Lemuel Haynes, Peter Salem, and Pomp Blackman. Lemuel Haynes was also at Fort Ticonderoga with the legendary Ethan Allen of Vermont's Green Mountain Boys as were Primas Black and Ephrem Blackman. Blacks also distinguished themselves at Bunker Hill. At a critical point in that battle, a British officer, Major Pitcairn, was exhorting his troops to charge. Peter Salem shot him and the British advance was repulsed. After the battle another Black patriot, Salem Poor, was singled out by his officers for commendation.

These early achievements and sacrifices of Blacks did little to enhance their acceptance into American society. When George Washington assumed command of the American forces, he quickly issued an order barring Negro participation in the war. His stated reason, despite evidence to the contrary, was that Blacks were inferior soldiers. This unfounded charge would stick to Black soldiers for years and wars to come. After the Revolutionary War it wasn't until the Korean War that Black soldiers were again given an equal opportunity to die in battle along with their White counterparts.

Washington's reluctance to use Black soldiers was understandable. Washington and most of his officers were from the South. Most were slave owners and were very familiar with the character of the American slave. They were reluctant to arm any Black man for any reason. However, events would soon force Washington to rescind his order. After a series of defeats, the Colonial forces settled into winter quarters at Valley Forge in December of 1777. Some 9,000 men accompanied Washington to Valley Forge. By March of 1778, three thousand had deserted and Washington was forced to take a hard look at the realities of his situation.

White men were not flocking to the cause. Enlistments were for relatively short periods of time. Many men felt no obligation to remain with the Army when planting time arrived back home. Those who could avoid service did so. Those who couldn't often paid others to take their places. Slave owners would substitute their slaves for themselves. By the time Washington broke camp and left Valley Forge, every patriot, Black or White, was welcomed in the Colonial Army.

In February of 1778, the Rhode Island legislature broke precedent and authorized the enlistment of Black troops. By the time the war ended, some 5,000 Blacks, slave and free, had taken part in the great quest for American freedom. Yet for many, freedom remained beyond their grasp. And that is one of the paradoxes of the American Revolution. Black men fought and died so that White men could be free. A classic example is that of Captain Mark Starlin, the Black Virginian Naval Captain. During the war he conducted daring raids on British vessels. After the war he was returned to his master. He died a slave.

Perhaps the greatest paradox of the American Revolution is its fundamental premise. The Declaration of Independence boldly proclaims:

> We hold these truths to be self evident, that all men are created equal, that they are endowed by their Creator with certain unalienable rights, that among these are Life, Liberty, and the pursuit of Happiness.

In Colonial Black America these stirring words rang hollow. They did not apply to the American slave. They applied only marginally for those Blacks who were free. Nevertheless, they were important. Once White America embraced the concept that "all men are created equal," it was inevitable that freedom for Black Americans would become a reality.

Thoughtful Americans could not dismiss the contradiction between their words and their actions. Soon after the signing of the Declaration of Independence, a *Rights of Man Movement* began to sweep across the country. People began to question the appropriateness of owning slaves. Some slave owners, such as Phillip Graham of Maryland, voluntarily freed their slaves. In 1777 the State of Vermont abolished slavery in its Constitution. Unfortunately, it would take almost one hundred years and a civil war before the words of the Declaration of Independence became a partial reality.

Although some 5,000 Blacks fought in the American Revolution little is remembered of their efforts. Images of that war are commemorated in the Minuteman statue on the green at Lexington and at the Concord Bridge. In the town hall in Marblehead, Massachusetts, there is a famous portrait *The Spirit of 1776*, depicting a flag bearer, a fife player, and a drummer boy. All are White! And another famous picture that appears in most history books is one of Washington crossing the Delaware. Prince Whipple and Oliver Cromwell, both Black, made that crossing with Washington, but neither are depicted in the portrait or mentioned in most texts.

Blacks from other countries also participated in the American Revolution, but they are rarely mentioned in history textbooks. While most Americans recognize the name of the Marquis de Lafayette as a French officer who volunteered to assist Washington, few recognize the Fontages Legion. The Fontages Legion was a Black unit sent from the French colony of Haiti to fight for the American cause.

Late in the Revolutionary War another Black man played a pivotal role in the success of White America's struggle against their British oppressors. James Armistead, acting as a spy for the Marquis de Lafayette, infiltrated the British position at Yorktown, Virginia. Armistead was so successful integrating himself among the British garrison that the British commander, General Charles Cornwallis, eventually asked Armistead to spy on the American forces. He happily accepted this task and henceforth moved between the two camps bringing valuable intelligence to the Americans and returning with false information for the British.

Slaves also served in the American Revolution. Some were sent in place of their masters. Others volunteered in hopes of being freed after the war. However, not all slaves were willing to fight for the American cause. Freedom could be obtained another way. The British commanders, most notably Lord Dunmore, offered freedom to slaves who would leave their masters and fight for the British. Many accepted the offer, and when the British forces finally departed American shores, they took some 20,000 Blacks with them. Some of the descendents of these slaves formed the African country of Sierra Leone.

❮

As the Revolutionary War came to a successful close, George Washington once again provided the setting for a final irony of the Black experience in the American Revolution. Military custom dictates that, before a unit changes command or is deactivated, the Commander assemble his officers for a final gathering Normally a meal is served and drinks are available. The highlight of the occasion is the Commander's farewell speech. It is a custom rich with tradition and requires the finest in food, drink and setting.

General Washington's farewell gathering was held in Fraunce's Tavern, one of New York City's most renowned eating establishments. The General who owned slaves and who had issued the order denying Blacks the right to fight for their country was the guest that evening of a Black restaurateur, Samuel Fraunce.

White America was free; the Revolution was over. It was now time to build a country. But what role would Blacks play? Would the principles of the Declaration of Independence apply to the approximately 697,000 slave and 59,000 free Blacks that were living in America. Unfortunately the answer was NO! Economics and politics would not allow it.

As the delegates met in Philadelphia to draft the new United States Constitution, two critical issues challenged them. First there was a strong feeling that slavery should be outlawed, but the political reality was that to get agreement on a Constitution a compromise had to be reached. It was finally agreed that the States could continue to import slaves until 1808. After that date the Congress would decide whether further importation of slaves would be allowed.

The second issue concerned representation and taxes. Southerners wanted representation to the House of Representatives based on the total population of their states, including their slaves. When it came to taxation, they did not want their slaves to be counted. Not surprisingly the Northerners wanted just the opposite. A compromise was reached that slaves would be counted as 3/5ths of a person. This agreement also compromised the concept that *all men are created equal* and formalized, in the mindset of White America, the idea of Black inferiority. Thus began a struggle in the American conscience that continues to this day.

Immediately following the Revolution, Blacks embarked on what Lerone Bennett calls in his book *Before the Mayflower* as the *Black Pioneer Period*.[4] Blacks were struggling to find their place in society. They were entering new fields of endeavor not previously experienced. Lemuel Haynes was pastor of a White church. Phyllis Wheatley published poetry. Benjamin Banneker became a mathematician. Emanuel and Mary Bernoon opened an oyster and alehouse in Providence, Rhode Island. James Forten acquired wealth as a sailmaker. For a time, as Black artisans and merchants emerged, it appeared that at least Free Blacks would live the American dream. But that was not to be the case. As the number of Free Blacks increased and competed for jobs, tensions rose in the major cities of the East. In New York and Boston

Blacks were the targets of insults and personal assaults. At the same time the invention of the cotton gin quashed any hopes that the principles of the Declaration of Independence would bring an end to slavery. Now cotton could be cleaned quicker and sold in greater quantities. More cotton was needed to meet demand, so new fields were planted and that required more slaves to pick the fields. The principles of the Revolution were not going to apply to Blacks, free or enslaved.

In this environment of rejection and repression, Blacks realized that they would have to rely on themselves to survive. In Philadelphia a group of eight men gathered to discuss their future as Black men in a White society. Among them were Richard Allen and Absalom Jones, and from this meeting emerged an organization to be known as The Free African Society. This organization acted as a buffer to protect all Blacks from the ill winds that were blowing around them. As similar organizations sprouted in other cities the framework was established for a separate Black society within that larger society known as the United States. This Black society would provide economic, political and social opportunity, but its fundamental roots were in the Black Church.

As in many other aspects of their lives Blacks initially sought to worship with their White brethren. At first there wasn't a problem, but as more Black faces occupied the pews Whites began to react. Lerone Bennett recounts a pivotal incident that led to the formation of the independent Black Church. He quotes from the recollections of Richard Allen. Allen was a prominent member of the Black community in the late 1700s. A former slave, he went on to become the first bishop of the African Methodist Episcopal Church.

Bennett quotes Allen in *Before the Mayflower* as recalling:

> A number of us usually attended St. George's church in Fourth Street; and when colored people began getting numerous in attending the church, they moved us from the seats we usually sat on, and placed us around the wall, and on Sabbath morning we went to church and the sexton stood at the door, and told us to go to the gallery . . . We expected to take the seats over the ones we occupied below, not knowing any better. . . . [M]eeting had begun and they were nearly done singing and just as we got to our seats, the

leader said, "Let us pray." We had not been long upon our knees before I heard considerable scuffling and low talking. I raised my head and saw one of the trustees . . . having hold of the Rev. Absalom Jones, pulling him off his knees, and saying, "You must get up—you must not kneel here." Mr. Jones replied "Wait until prayer is over." The trustee said, "No, you must get up now, or I will call for aid and force you away." Mr. Jones said, "Wait until prayer is over, and I will get up and trouble you no more." With that the trustee beckoned to one of the other trustees . . . to come to his assistance. He came and went to William White to pull him up. By this time prayer was over, and we all went out of church in a body, and they were no more plagued with us in that church.

The Mr. Jones referred to in this incident was Absalom Jones, a co-founder of The Free African Society, a protest leader and the founder of one of the first Black churches in the North. Following this incident Richard Allen formed the independent Black Methodist Church and in 1816 became the first Bishop of The African Methodist Episcopal Church. In 1821 James Varick organized the African Methodist Episcopal Zion Church. By the 1830s there were Black churches of many denominations.

In the Black Pioneer Period Richard Allen, Absalom Jones, and other political and religious leaders established a link between the church and the community that has been passed on through generations. It is not a coincidence that through the years the Black community has looked to the church for its leadership. The church and its ministers have provided and continue to provide a haven for the Black community in times of joy, tragedy, and everyday living.

The Black quest for equal rights is also rooted in the period immediately following the American Revolution. Richard Allen, Absalom Jones, Prince Hall, and many others petitioned the Congress and various state legislatures on subjects ranging from the abolition of slavery to better education for their children. One ironic case involved Paul Cuffe. Cuffe was a Black ship builder and sea captain who would put to sea with a

Black crew and travel to ports as distant as Russia and Africa. In 1780 Cuffe went to vote in his hometown of Dartmouth, Massachusetts. He was denied. His response was to refuse to pay his taxes reminding the officials of that cradle and citadel of liberty, Massachusetts, that *taxation without representation* was wrong. He was allowed to vote.

While Blacks in the North struggled to find their place in society, there was no such dilemma in the South. In the cotton states the divisions between Black and White were clearly defined. Whites were the masters and Blacks were the slaves. White was superior. Black was inferior. And from these divisions emerged attitudes and beliefs that continue to plague both races in the 21st Century.

☾

Slavery is an unpleasant word. It carries with it not only negative connotations, but visions of people being whipped, being chained together, working in intolerable conditions, and living apart from family. It is not a word that the business community of Colonial America found palatable. And yet it was a reality of the cotton business and would at times become a point of issue when negotiating price in a transaction. A buyer arguing that the price should be lowered because of the seller's reduced labor costs would be careful not to offend his compatriot. He could hardly come right out and say that slave labor had saved the planter considerable costs in production and therefore justified a lower selling price. He made his point by substituting a euphemism for the word slavery. Slavery was referred to as the *Peculiar Institution*. And indeed it was a peculiar institution.

In the South the majority of the slaves worked on plantations. In many cases the plantations were not much more than farms with small numbers of slaves. However, there were large plantations with many slaves and many fields to pick. Mount Vernon, George Washington's home in Virginia, is a classic example of a large plantation.

The classic plantation was an independent self-sustaining business

On larger plantations slave quarters were lined in rows as shown above. Each cabin was no more than a one-room shack. *Image courtesy of Documentary Photo Aids.*

organization. A product was produced. To ensure the ability to get the product to market, many plantations were located near or on a river. There was a main house for the master and his family, smaller quarters for administrative personnel, a blacksmith shop, a cookhouse, barns, and other buildings for animals and equipment. The quarters for the slaves, commonly referred to as slave row, were more remotely placed. Food was grown in sufficient quantity and variety to feed the planter's family and provide for the labor force. And finally, there were the fields for growing the product for the slaves to pick.

A large plantation had its own society. At the top were the master and his family. In many cases the family had little direct involvement with the daily affairs of running the plantation. That was the primary responsibility of the overseer, a White employee who was the plantation's business manager. He was responsible for the business of making a profit and was given the authority necessary to complete his task. His authority included the management and discipline of his labor force, the slaves.

Below the overseer was the Head Driver. The driver was a slave whose function was to supervise the other slaves. It was the driver who held reveille in the morning, made certain the slaves were in the fields on time, supervised their work, checked their daily quota, and returned the slaves to their quarters when the day's work was done. The driver also reported infractions of discipline to the overseer and at times administered some punishments. The most basic punishment, 30 lashes with the whip, was generally administered by the overseer or the master.

The driver was the most important and most despised Negro on the plantation. He had separate quarters and was given privileges in the form of food, some freedom, an occasional bottle of liquor, and female companionship. But his was not an envious life. He was usually assigned the job whether he wanted it or not. Sometimes a planter would go to a slave auction for the specific purpose of purchasing a male slave to use as a driver. The driver had few friends and knew that if he displeased the overseer he would be sent to the fields and made to live with the other slaves, an uninviting prospect at best.

There were several groupings of slaves on the plantation. House slaves were assigned to the main house and performed such tasks as cooks, maids, butlers, and carriage drivers. These slaves were in constant contact with the master and his family. This closeness could be both a blessing and a curse. Generally the house slaves had better clothing and food, but they had little freedom by virtue of their close contact with the family. Some family members became quite attached to the house slaves who acted as their personal servants. This was particularly true of the *Mammy*.

Mammy was the slave who was in charge of the White children. In many cases Mammy had more to do with raising the children than did their natural mother. The relationship of love and affection of the Mammy for her White children and vice versa was one of the most complex and hard to understand relationships in slavery. Adult men and women who professed love for their Mammy could at the same time consider her a piece of property and as an inferior being who required their self-indulgent protection.

The majority of the plantation's slave population worked in the fields. Field slaves—men and women, young and old—were expected to be in the fields at the crack of dawn and remain there often until well after the sun had set. They usually had a break of about twenty minutes for lunch. Children who had reached the age of six were required to go to the fields. They would carry water

Slaves worked in the fields from sun-up to sunset. Picking cotton was back-breaking work. *Image courtesy of Documentary Photo Aids.*

and food or do other menial chores. It was a kind of acclimation period, which prepared them for the task of picking once they reached the age of 12 or 13. While their parents were in the field, the very young children were put under the care of a slave woman known as *Nanny*.

When the day's fieldwork was done, the slaves were returned to their cabins on slave row. Their work still wasn't done as they now cooked their evening meal and completed the normal daily chores of their personal lives. Late at night they would finally go to sleep in preparation for repeating the cycle the next day. Their homes were generally a one-room cabin with a dirt floor. The whole family lived there and every aspect of their lives—birth, sickness, joy, sadness, and death—took place in that shack.

Twice a year slaves were issued clothing. In the fall they each received

This picture shows slaves on a Southern plantation in approximately 1862. In the background is a typical slave cabin. *Image courtesy of Documentary Photo Aids.*

two cotton shirts, one pair of woolen pants and a woolen jacket and in the spring two cotton shirts and two pairs of cotton pants. Women received materials and sewing utensils to make the clothes they required. Each slave got a pair of shoes each year and a woolen blanket every third year.[9]

Food was issued weekly and generally included corn, salt pork, or bacon. Slaves supplemented the food supply by hunting and farming small plots that the master allowed them to cultivate. They also supplemented their food by appropriating anything they could from the master's stores and from his garbage. Scraps of meat—such as the tongue, intestines, brains, and feet of pigs—were turned into edible dishes by the slaves. Today's delicacy known as chitlins is a product of the ingenuity of the slaves in preparing pigs' intestines. Taking from the master was acceptable in the slaves' eyes. But taking the property of another slave was stealing and not acceptable at all.[10]

There was a natural competition between the house slaves and the field slaves. Being better dressed and working in better conditions, house slaves would sometimes put on airs and look down at the less fortunate field slave. On the other hand field slaves often regarded the house slaves as uppity. Neither cared to change places with the other and this played to the master's benefit. Next to the lash the most unappealing punishment for either would be to be placed in the house or in the field. The house slave could not adjust to the grueling work in the hot sun, and the field slave hated the loss of freedom the field provided and feared the prospect of being under the master's watchful eye.

❛

Most slaves lived in families headed by a mother and a father. The slave owners did not respect the nuclear family and family members were often sold off separately. Worse, the practice of breeding slaves and selling them further eroded the concept of family. However, the slaves were bound together by their common experience. From this experience developed the concept that all slaves were members of one big extended family. That today's Blacks refer to one another as brother and sister is an outgrowth of this tradition.

A slave marriage was truly a love match. The man and woman were equal in all respects. They both worked and shared the rigors of slavery. Neither one had any material goods. There was no such thing as a dowry. Also there was no need to marry simply to satisfy sexual desires. Premarital sex was accepted in the slave rows. Finally, marrying and raising a family was a risky endeavor. Slaves could be and were sold with little regard for their emotions, family ties, children or any other personal considerations. It is impressive that the slaves were willing to accept the responsibilities and risks of marriage despite these obstacles.[11]

The marriage ceremony was relatively simple. The two individuals would appear before one of the elders who would ask them if they wished to be joined together. On receipt of an affirmative answer, the elder would place a broomstick on the ground and direct the couple to jump over it. Having done so, the couple was then considered married. It was important to jump high and not stumble if the marriage was to get off to a smooth start.

Life on slave row was not much different from life among any grouping of peoples. There were standards of conduct accepted by the group. Children were raised, traditions from the African past were preserved, and customs from their present situation were established. A distinct society was created. Within this society leaders emerged, many of whom were women.

Not all life was drudgery. Generally slaves were not required to work on Sundays, and that left Saturday night as a time for relaxation and socializing. On occasion, there would be dances and partying with banjo music and singing adding to the enjoyment. From the slave row came rhythms and sounds that form the basis of much of America's historical and contemporary musical traditions: gospel, blues, jazz, and eventually rock and roll.

Religion played an important role in the lives of the slaves. Try as they might, the masters were never able to completely eradicate the religious customs, traditions, and beliefs in the spirits that accompanied the slaves on their journey from Africa. The slaves were partially introduced to a Christianity that suited the White man's purpose. They were told that the Bible, God's word, said: "Obey your master." They were assured that, although their lives were Hell on earth, good slaves would reap their reward in Heaven.

Most slaves were unable to read and could not dispute what was presented as God's word. However, some could and understood that the God of the Bible sent Moses to lead the slaves out of Egypt. The word was spread from plantation to plantation in secret meetings and by word of mouth. Soon the God of the Israelites became the hope of the American slave. The spiritual beliefs of Africa and the benevolent God of the Israelites merged in the slave rows of the Southern plantations and from it came the roots of the Black Church we know today.[12]

❨

Myth has it that the slaves were content with their situation. The smiling, deferential slaves depicted in too many Hollywood films distort the truth. Slaves continually resisted their masters. They conducted work slow downs, broke tools, and resisted in any way they could. Some house slaves went so far as to poison their masters or add such delicacies as ground glass to their food. A favorite means of resistance was setting fire to crops. And of course the slaves ran away.

Controlling the slaves was a major concern of the planters. After all, the slaves on any given plantation outnumbered the Whites. It was essential that they be controlled and prevented from planning or executing a revolt. There were too many documented incidents of slaves killing their masters to overlook the necessity for security. Laws were passed in each slave state known as Slave Codes. These codes were designed to keep slaves ignorant and in awe of Whites. Foremost was the law making it a crime to teach a slave to read. Other laws prohibited slaves from gathering in groups of more than five or leaving the plantation without a pass. And every White person had police power over every Black.

The slave codes were further designed to control the slaves by brainwashing. The object of brainwashing was to accomplish two goals. The first was to make the slaves believe they should be slaves. The second was to convince them that they were powerless to change their situation. An essential element for successful brainwashing was to ensure that the slaves never saw a White man who did not command their respect. The slaves must always be in a position where they felt inferior to the White man. Poor uneducated Whites were plentiful in the South. In many cases their situations were not much better than the slaves. It was important that the slaves not associate or identify with these Whites. By these and other means the slave owners attempted to reduce the possibility of slave revolts.[13]

❨

The owners failed. Although they succeeded in individual cases, they were unable to brainwash a whole race. The instinct to be free was too strong, and slaves continually revolted during their captivity. Unfortunately, most revolts failed. Only one truly succeeded and that occurred outside of the United States in 1791 in the French colony of Haiti. On August 22, 1791 the Haitian slaves rose up, slew their masters and claimed their freedom.

Several factors entered into the success of the Haitian slaves. Their revolt was well planned and coordinated. The essential element of surprise was complete. At the time the French planters in Haiti were distracted by the events of the French Revolution back home. The planters had adopted their revolution's slogan *Liberté, Egalité, Fraternité* and spoke openly of their grievances with their King. These Frenchmen never dreamed that their slaves understood their conversations or shared their grievances. They considered their slaves more as children than as mature, rational, understanding men and women. But the slaves listened, understood, and planned.

Planning was a key ingredient for the successful Haitian Revolution, and the planters themselves had unwittingly assisted their slaves. Being a Catholic colony, the French had allowed the slaves more freedom than their English counterparts in the United States. Haitian slaves were allowed to keep many of their native customs. In particular, they were allowed their music with its drums. Drums, however, provide a significant means of communication and were used to transmit the messages necessary for a coordinated attack. Meanwhile the French planters hearing the drums gave them scant notice.

As the Haitian slaves set fire to their plantations, the French, English, and Spanish were warring against each other for control of the island. The instability of the situation was ideal for the slaves to use to their advantage. After their initial successes the Haitian slaves needed a strong leader to consolidate their gains. At this point a 52 year-old slave, whose most important previous position had been that of a carriage driver, entered the scene. His name was François Dominique Toussaint L'Ouverture. He would become the George Washington of Haiti.

With the assistance of L'Ouverture and his guerrilla army, the French successfully thwarted Spanish and English ambitions for the island. By the end of these conflicts, L'Ouverture had consolidated the gains of the slaves' revolt and in fact ruled the island in the name of France. He now exhibited extraordinary administrative ability in governing Haiti. Recognizing that he could accomplish little without the political and economic expertise of the White population, he was quick to make an accommodation with the former masters, assuring them they would not be harmed if they would remain on the island and cooperate with his administration. Soon Blacks and Whites alike held him in the highest esteem.

The French Emperor, Napoleon Bonaparte, was not a man to relinquish power easily. He had planned to use Haiti as a base to expand French influence in North America. L'Ouverture's assumption of power in Haiti thwarted Naepoleon's ambitions for expansion. Therefore, he sent General Victor Leclerc and an army of some 25,000 soldiers to remove L'Ouverture. A brutal campaign followed. It ended after one of L'Ouverture's top aides, Henri Christophe, defected to the enemy. After Christope's defection L'Ouverture sued for a truce.

With the war at an end, L'Ouverture retired to his plantation. In the eyes of the French, however, he remained a threat that must be eliminated. Subsequently, the French commander, under the guise of good will, invited L'Ouverture to visit his headquarters for a discussion of conditions in Haiti. On arriving at the French headquarters, L'Ouverture was arrested and sent to France in chains. He died in a French prison in 1803.[14]

Having thus disposed of L'Ouverture, the French faced a new problem. His name was Jean Jacques Dessalines. Dessalines was a former slave who hated all Frenchmen. He had been a trusted assistant of L'Overture and was considered a military genius. Dessalines completed the only successful slave revolt in North America when in November of 1803 he defeated Napoleon's forces at Vertieres. After the French surrendered Dessalines took the French Tricolor and tore the white from it re-stitching the red and blue panels together. There would be no White in the Haitian flag.[15]

The Haitian Revolution had an immediate and a long-term impact on America. As Whites fled Haiti and brought news of the revolt to the United States, fear gripped the American slave owners and caused them to tighten security over their slaves. Slave codes were expanded, discipline tightened, and life became more unbearable for the American slave. It also became a nightmare for the planters and their families, as visions of rampaging slaves filled their nightly dreams. For the American slave the Haitian Revolution brought hope and provided a model to emulate. Finally, as a result of the Haitian Revolution and its costs in men, money and materials, Napoleon lost interest in further expansion in the Americas and agreed to the Louisiana Purchase with the United States government. America doubled its size as a result of this purchase.

The United States and Haiti have had a long history that has united the two countries. Haitians fought in the American Revolution for the Colonies against the British. The ideals of the American Revolution, equality and liberty, influenced the Haitian slaves in their revolt. The bond of slavery is shared by Haitians and African Americans. All these factors have left an invisible bond between the two countries that is perpetuated today. American support of President Jean-Bertrand Aristide in the 1990s can be traced to the Fontages Legion of the American Revolution.

☾

The successful slave revolt in Haiti was the exception. Revolts in the United States generally met with failure for a variety of reasons, not the least of which was betrayal of the plans by fellow slaves. In the summer of 1800, Gabriel Prosser, a deeply religious slave, planned to take over the State of Virginia and make it a Black state with him as its ruler. He planned a three pronged attack on Richmond after which his forces would spread out and take the rest of the State. On the night of the attack on Richmond, there was a storm. The fields and roads were flooded and all but impassable. Rather than take advantage of the terrible weather, which would have increased the element of surprise and created even more confusion, Prosser postponed his attack. Meanwhile, he was betrayed by other slaves who revealed his plan to the authorities. Before he could resume his attack, Prosser was captured and subsequently hung. Had he not delayed, Gabriel Prosser could well have been successful, a fact that did not escape White Virginians. As word of Prosser's plan spread the South was once again gripped with fear.

☾

Denmark Vesey was a former slave who had bought his freedom after winning a lottery. His wife and son were slaves. He was a carpenter and an astute businessman in Charleston, South Carolina. While a slave, as a boy, Vesey had spent time at sea and had learned the skills of a seafarer, particularly navigation. In 1821 Vesey plotted to take over the city of Charleston, capture the ships in port, and use them to transport all the slaves he could gather to freedom in Haiti. The revolt was to occur on Sunday, July 16, 1822. Success was dependent on surprise and the ability to take control of the arsenal and the port. If necessary, the plan called for killing all Whites who stood in the way including the plotters' masters, among whom was the Governor of South Carolina.

Vesey planned his revolt for over a year. His status as a free man added credibility in his effort to recruit followers. After all he had as much, if not more, to lose than those he was asking to join him. His free status and his outspoken manner, however, earned him the enmity and jealousy of some slaves. This would eventually lead to his undoing. Nevertheless, Vesey was careful in his planning. Only a few loyal assistants, such as Peter Poyas, were entrusted with the details of the plan. Others

37

were provided information only on a need to know basis. Despite these safeguards a house slave, who informed his master of the time and date of the revolt, betrayed Vesey and his fellow plotters. Vesey and his accomplices were arrested and hung. The unveiling of Denmark Vesey's plan sent shock waves through the Charleston community. Whites vowed to never again be without adequate protection. In the years that followed, increased emphasis was placed on military protection, and in 1842 a military institution was founded, known today as The Citadel.

Denmark Vesey's revolt was a success despite its failure. The world could no longer pretend that the American Negro was content to be a slave. Here was a free man who was willing to risk his life so his wife and son could be free. Here was a free man who would forfeit his life to free people he didn't even know from a system of brutal repression. Here was a man whose failure spoke eloquently against injustice.

Gabriel Prosser and Denmark Vesey were each betrayed by other slaves before they could complete their missions. How could that happen? Why would any slave betray a plan for freedom? These are logical questions, but they overlook one essential consideration. The slaves were human beings and as such had hopes, dreams, fears, and emotions like any human beings. They were not one homogeneous group. Granted most shared a common goal of obtaining their freedom, but not all were willing to risk death to achieve it. Similarly, their White masters were human beings as well. They too were not a homogeneous group, and there were sharp divisions among them as to the treatment of the slaves. After Vesey's plot was revealed, some masters could not conceive that their slaves would kill them. However, once that realization took root, life for the remaining slaves became more difficult, at least in South Carolina.

The revolts of Denmark Vesey and Gabriel Prosser were thwarted before they started. Whites feared what could have happened, but no blood was shed. Nat Turner's revolt shed blood.

《

Nat Turner was born in 1800. At five feet six inches he was not a physically large man, but he was indeed large. He was a charismatic slave and deeply religious. The story is told that Nat converted his overseer and convinced him to change his ways, much to the chagrin of the local Whites who in turn forced the overseer out of town.[16] Turner believed that God had selected him to kill the enemies of his people. In August, 1831 that is exactly what Turner set out to do.

Unlike Prosser and Vesey, Turner did not plan extensively. Rather, he gathered a small force, and starting with his master's farm he proceeded to kill every White in his path from Cabin Pond, Virginia, to Jerusalem, Virginia. Along the way other slaves joined the murderous group until they numbered about 70. At Jerusalem, a superior force of Whites stopped Turner's advance and he was forced to flee. He returned to Cabin Pond, went into hiding, and was able to escape capture for about two months.

While Nat Turner hid, Southampton County, Virginia, was the scene of panic and retribution. The slightest rumor that Nat was approaching sent Whites fleeing. Meanwhile soldiers combed the countryside searching for Nat, indiscriminately killing slaves as they went. Some justified the actions of the soldiers as a preventive measure for prospective terrorists. The number of slaves killed is unknown. Nat was eventually captured and hung on November 11, 1831, approximately 30 years before the first shot of the Civil War was fired at Fort Sumter.

The wanton killing and sheer brutality of Nat's rampage through Southampton County forced thoughtful Americans to question what kind of system could breed such violence. They concluded that the system itself was violent. Turner's bloody revolt had finally provided the impetus for the Abolitionist Movement and set the wheels in motion that would eventually lead to the Civil War.

NOTES

1. Lerone Bennett Jr. *Before the Mayflower; A History of Black America* (New York: Penguin, 1987), p. 29

5. Bennett, pp. 37-40

6. Bennett, p. 61

7. Bennett, p. 65

8. Bennett, p. 70

9. Bennett, pp. 89-90

10. Bennett, p. 89

11. Bennett, pp. 106-107

12. Bennett, p. 99

13. Bennett, p. 109

14. Bennet, p. 123

15. Bennett, p. 124

16. Bennett, p. 134

3

Abolitionist Movement through Reconstruction

Nat Turner's bloody rampage through Southampton County, Virginia, ignited a series of events that culminated in war and left a legacy of a nation divided along color lines. Turner forced the issue into the open. Was slavery acceptable or not? The question had been on peoples' minds for a long time.

If all men are created equal, how could we justify keeping some men slaves? For the purist the answer was simple. We couldn't. However, to many, the problem was far more complex. The Southern planter's livelihood depended on a stable work force. The Northern shipbuilder needed the demand for his product that the slave trade provided. Men whose economic survival depended on slavery were generally unwilling to consider the abolition of that institution on the basis of moral arguments. Americans were caught in a vexing dilemma, one they would struggle with for 30 years after the capture and hanging of Old Nat.

Gradual emancipation of the slaves had already been suggested, based on moral and religious arguments, by anti-slavery groups. In 1820 Benjamin Lundy, a Quaker, was publishing an anti-slavery newspaper which appealed to the public's moral instincts as a means of attacking slavery. One solution that gained popularity, and was supported by men like Lundy, was put forward by the American Colonization Society. The goals of this society included returning Free Blacks to Africa and buying the freedom of as many slaves as possible in order to return them to Africa as well.[17] As a means of accomplishing these goals the Society established the West African country of Liberia.

Colonization of the Free Blacks was a particularly appealing prospect to the slave owner. Free Blacks, like Denmark Vesey, were a constant irritant. In the first place they were living proof of the lie of "Black Inferiority." Here were men and women who demonstrated daily that Blacks were very capable of living successful lives if left to their own initiatives. Secondly, they were an inspiration, a living example, for slaves to seek their freedom. As such, they were a problem to be eliminated. What better way than by exportation?

Colonization, as a solution to the problem of a Black and White America, was seriously considered as early as 1771. Thomas Jefferson advocated the idea in a paper entitled *Notes on the State of Virginia*.[18] Abraham Lincoln had embraced the concept before he arrived in Washington. Later in the summer prior to issuing his famous Emancipation Proclamation, Lincoln met in the White House with selected Black leaders. After expressing his belief that it was not in the interest of either race to live together, he proposed the relocation of Free Blacks to Central America. Again as late as 1865, Lincoln was still seriously considering colonization when he asked Ben Butler, a former Union general, to conduct a study on the feasibility of deporting the newly freed slaves to another land.

The Colonization Movement never did truly catch hold, primarily because Blacks resisted all efforts to force them from their country. By the 1800s Blacks had been in America for close to 200 years. They had fought in the American Revolution. They had buried their parents and welcomed their newborn. They had raised families. Many Free Blacks had established themselves and were financially secure. They considered themselves Americans. Africa had no appeal for them.

Free Blacks also knew that if they left this country, the lives of their brothers and sisters in bondage would be worse and the opportunity of ending slavery would be greatly diminished. One of the most strident opponents of the Colonization Movement was James Forten. Forten was an independent businessman who operated a sail making shop. At one time he employed more than 40 workers, Black and White. He was not only against colonization; he was also an abolitionist. As early as 1800, Forten, along with the Reverend Richard Allen, circulated a petition calling for the U.S. Congress to emancipate the slaves.

There was a time, immediately following the American Revolution, when it appeared that slavery would come to a natural end. The public conscience had embraced the principles of the American Revolution. People were talking about a *Rights of Man Movement.* Many believed that all men were in fact equal and should be treated accordingly. For a time, men like Phillip Graham of Maryland voluntarily freed their slaves, and for a moment it appeared that the curse of slavery would be lifted from the country.[19] Unfortunately, Eli Whitney invented his cotton gin.

The invention of the cotton gin created an immediate need for more slaves. Now that cotton could be cleaned faster, greater quantities could be sold. Production was increased. More fields were planted. More slaves were needed to plant and pick. The Rights of Man Movement gave way to economic necessity and emancipation became a distant memory until Nat Turner killed his master.

Nat Turner provided the spark, but a multitude of Black and White men and women fanned the flames of abolition. Henry Highland Garnett and Sojourner Truth spoke eloquently against the evils of slavery. William Lloyd Garrison attacked slavery in his newspaper *The Liberator.* David Ruggles and Harriet Tubman used the Underground Railroad as their means of bringing slavery to an end.

Hundreds of faceless men and women, knowing full well the consequences of failure, expressed their opinion about slavery by voting with their feet. These were the *Running Abolitionists*, the brave slaves who dared to run away, who used their feet and personal fortitude to claim their freedom. And fortitude was indeed necessary. Bounty hunters and bloodhounds pursued them.

After the passage of the Fugitive Slave Law in 1850, there was no safe place to hide. This law required local and state officials to aid federal officials in the capture and return of runaway slaves. A captured runaway could expect severe punishment for attempting to flee and also as a deterrent for potential runaways.

❰

In addition to the Running Abolitionists there were other categories of abolitionists. *Talking Abolitionists* like Frederick Douglass and Sojourner Truth wrote and spoke against slavery. *Active Abolitionists* such as Harriet Tubman took action to directly attack slavery.

Sojourner Truth is one of the more colorful characters among the abolitionists. She was born Isabella Baumfree into slavery about 1797, was married, and had six children. In 1827 she was emancipated under New York State law. About this time her youngest son, Peter, was sold into slavery. With the help of some Quaker friends, she successfully filed suit to obtain his freedom. In 1843 she believed God spoke to her telling her to travel throughout the country talking against slavery. It was at this time that she

Sojourner Truth: preacher, abolitionist, and lecturer. *Image courtesy of Documentary Photo Aids.*

changed her name to Sojourner Truth. A tall, imposing woman with a deep voice, Sojourner captivated audiences as she spoke out against the evils of slavery. Later in her life she became a leader in the Women's Rights Movement.

Frederick Douglass escaped from slavery at the age of 21. By then he had learned two valuable lessons. When he was about 16, Douglass had been sent by his master to be "tamed," a common practice for recalcitrant youths. The tamer in this case was a man named Edward Covey. After receiving several beatings, Douglass

Frederick Douglass. *Image courtesy of Documentary Photo Aids.*

refused to take any more. Thereafter, whenever Covey would attempt to punish him, Douglass would prevent it by knocking Covey to the ground. Since this sufficiently discouraged Covey, the beatings ceased. From this experience Douglass realized that "when a slave cannot be whipped he is more than half free. Men are whipped oftenest who are whipped easiest." A few years later Douglass was hired out by his master to work in a Baltimore shipyard. His experience there was unpleasant. Whites who resented working next to a slave beat him. More important was the fact that his master took all his wages. These experiences made Douglass question why he was a slave. He concluded that he could be no worse off if he died trying to escape to freedom. Douglass, disguised as a sailor, ran away on September 3, 1838.

Douglass was 21 years old when he escaped and fled to New York. Shortly thereafter he married a Free Black whom he had previously been dating in Baltimore and the couple moved to Massachusetts. Soon Douglass was speaking at Abolitionist gatherings. He was a natural orator, and having once been a slave, he captivated his audiences by his vivid description of life as a slave.

In 1845 Douglass was in London. Since England had abolished slavery in 1834, Black Abolitionists were very popular speakers. Douglass was particularly popular and traveled throughout England with his abolitionist message. His speeches increased the anti-slavery sentiments of the English people. Later, the English peoples' abhorrence of slavery would have a profound affect on the outcome of the Civil War.

In the 1800s, England was spearheading the Industrial Revolution in Europe and was a leading manufacturer of textiles. At the onset of the American Civil War, the English government was considering supporting the Confederacy with weapons, ammunition, and very possibly their Navy in exchange for the cotton they needed to feed their textile mills. Such an arrangement would have been of significant value to the South as it lacked the manufacturing base to sustain a prolonged war. The English government, however, knew that the anti-slavery sentiments of the English people would never stand for such an arrangement. Rather than risk a vote of no confidence, the English government opted to seek its source of cotton elsewhere. Thus the Confederacy was denied much needed industrial and military resources. Had the English allied with the Confederacy, the outcome of the Civil War and the subsequent history of the world could have been dramatically different.

While a slave, Douglass had been taught to read by his master's wife. On learning of his wife's indiscretion, the master immediately put an end to this effort. Nevertheless, Douglass did learn to read and came to appreciate the power of an education. Later in his role as the most distinguished abolitionist of his day, Douglass repeatedly emphasized the importance of education.

In the first half of the 19th century, as immigrants from Europe streamed into the United States, Douglass believed that education was particularly necessary for Free Blacks. He watched as White immigrants, willing to work for low wages, began taking over service jobs that had been traditionally the domain of the Blacks. Whites were now working as porters, house servants, dockers, barbers, etc. In March, 1853, in an effort to make his brethren understand the danger before them, Douglass published an editorial entitled *Learn Trades or Starve*. Nevertheless, learning a trade was not easily accomplished. Many craft unions excluded Blacks and in some cases it was against the law to teach Blacks a trade.

Active Abolitionists were people who directly attacked slavery. Harriet Tubman is the classic example. After escaping slavery, she returned to the South nineteen times and helped more than 300 slaves to escape. She took pride in saying of her Underground Railroad experience: "I nebber run my train off de track and I nebber lost a passenger." During the Civil War Tubman provided valuable service as a spy for the Union Army.

❦

There was another group of abolitionists who have remained unnamed in history, but who deserve more than a passing mention since they truly were heroes. Their heroism stems from the fact that they never planned to be abolitionists, but when faced with a difficult decision they made a brave choice.

Imagine it is a cold, rainy November evening and you and your family have just begun the evening meal when there is a knock at the door. On opening the door, you come face to face with a gaunt shivering woman. Behind her, at the bottom of the porch steps, are a man and two small children. The woman is clearly frightened as she explains that they are escaping slaves who are being pursued by bounty hunters. She then asks you to hide them.

Many a husband and wife were faced with this dilemma. If they helped, they could put themselves, their family, and their possessions in danger. They could even be breaking the law. If they refused, the fate of those poor souls on their doorstep would remain on their conscience. Abolition, in this instance, was no longer a theory to be debated. It was a reality to be faced.

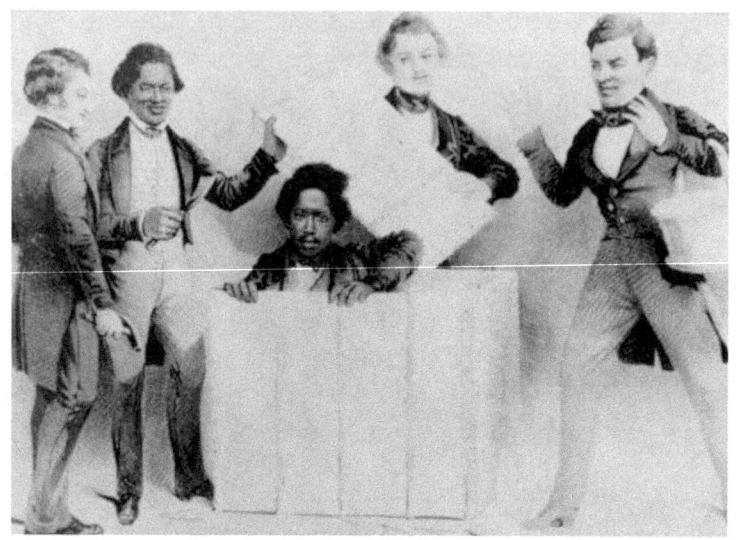

Henry "Box" Brown escaped slavery by being shipped as merchandise. Brown started his odyssey in Richmond, Virginia. Twenty-six hours later the Adams Express Company delivered him to Philadelphia and freedom. *Image courtesy of Documentary Photo Aids.*

❆

Slaves were ingenious in devising means of escape. Henry Brown of Richmond, Virginia, hid in a box that he had shipped to Philadelphia. Henceforth, he was known as "Box" Brown. Ellen Craft, who was almost White, posed as a sickly gentleman traveling North for medical attention. She was accompanied by her husband William, acting as her loyal slave and servant. Traveling by boat and train, they successfully reached Philadelphia and eventually moved to Boston. After the passage of the Fugitive Slave Law, the Crafts moved to England, returning only after the Civil War ended. However, it was the Underground Railroad that caught the imagination of the public and has overshadowed the escapes of people like "Box" Brown and the Crafts.

The Underground Railroad, the best-known abolitionist activity, is surrounded by legend and myth. Those who assisted escaping slaves were the *conductors*. Places where slaves were hidden overnight were the *stations*. One almost gets the impression that there were tracks throughout the South to carry the slaves to freedom. Quite the contrary is true. The railroad was operated primarily in the North, as few abolitionists were willing to risk the dangers of going into the South and guiding slaves to freedom. Harriet Tubman and Josiah Henson were exceptions. The railroad was more a series of regional activities than any national organization. It was also an effort more inspired by the actions of individuals rather than of organizations. The popular conception that the Quakers sponsored the Underground Railroad probably arose from the fact that two of the more famous abolitionists who assisted fugitive slaves, Levi Coffin and Thomas Garrett, were Quakers.

Legend wraps the activities of the Underground Railroad in secrecy. In fact, the activities and sympathies of men like Coffin and Garrett were no secret in their communities. Nevertheless, the danger inherent in assisting runaway slaves did demand a degree of secrecy. Houses with secret rooms and passageways where slaves were hidden can still be found today throughout the North.

After passage of the Fugitive Slave Law in 1793, slaves were no longer safe simply by crossing the Mason-Dixon Line. Now they had to reach Canada to be truly free. The support and guidance of the people who were willing to open their hearts and homes to the Running Abolitionists was more necessary than ever before. It is conservatively estimated that from 1850 to 1860 approximately 1,000 slaves ran away each year.[20]

❮

Abolition was a word that incited men and women to extremes. They were either for or against it. Those opposed to abolition were clear in their opposition. They knew the stakes and were unswerving in their resolve. Those advocating abolition, although equally fervent in their resolve, couldn't seem to come together under one banner. This division of ideas can be seen in the break between William Lloyd Garrison, the fiery editor of *The Liberator*, and Frederick Douglass. Each of these men despised the evil of slavery. Douglass had lived as a slave. Garrison, who was White, found it morally repugnant. Nevertheless, they couldn't agree on the best way to attack it.

Garrison believed that speeches, editorials, political pressure, and passive resistance were the appropriate courses of action. Douglass believed that those measures weren't enough. As time went by and he came in contact with militant abolitionists like John Brown, Douglass reached the conclusion that the elimination of slavery would ultimately require the use of force. Douglass also believed that Black men should be leading the fight against slavery, not well-intentioned White men.

On these basic issues Douglass split with Garrison and found himself more closely allied with the philosophy of the more militant Samuel Ringold Ward of New York. Thus the abolitionists divided into two camps with those following Douglass known as the New Yorkers and those more inclined to Garrison's ideas known as the Garrisonians. This split among the abolitionists continued until the South's decision to shell Fort Sumter made it a moot point.

❈

During the period immediately following the American Revolution until the beginning of the Civil War, jobs became the focal point for conflict between Black Americans and Americans of other hues and nationalities. Two circumstances were responsible. First, the Rights of Man Movement increased the number of Free Blacks competing for jobs. Second, the Immigration Movement increased the pool of available unskilled and skilled White workers. Having a job was fundamental to survival of Blacks and immigrants alike.

Most of the immigrants reaching the shores of the United States came from European backgrounds. They were naturally assimilated into society by those who had preceded them. It was a natural phenomenon for Irish, Italian, German, and Jewish communities to sprout in American cities. It was equally natural for these ethnic groups to look out for each other and find work for one another. Blacks, on the other hand, were different. They had arrived as slaves. They were only beginning to establish a cohesive society in America. They were viewed with fear, suspicion, and disdain. They were a problem.

The solution to the problem of Black competition for jobs was, in the early 19th century, exclusion and prejudice. That solution became embedded in America culture, has been passed from generation to generation, and has been particularly difficult to uproot. The Civil Rights Movement of the 1950s and 1960s and the controversial Affirmative Action Program of the 1980s and 1990s were necessary results of attitudes and prejudices spawned by economic circumstances prior to the Civil War.

While the Abolitionist Movement is most often highlighted when studying the years leading up to the Civil War, it is important to understand that during these years Black Americans were developing in other areas as well. Despite resistance at every turn, Free Blacks were enrolling in secondary schools across the nation. By 1850 there were some fourteen hundred Black students in the Baltimore schools and another thousand in New Orleans.

Blacks had even ventured into the hallowed halls of higher education. In 1823, Alexander Twilight received a degree from Middlebury College in Vermont and became the first Black to receive a college degree in the United States. Middlebury College continued its tradition of leadership in Black affairs when in the 1960s one of its undergraduates, Cecil Forrester, enrolled in the U.S. Marine Corps Platoon Leaders Class and went on to become one of the Corps' first Black lawyers. In 1826, Edward Jones and John Russwurm graduated from Amherst and Bowdin Colleges respectively.

Freedom's Journal, the first Black newspaper, was published in New York City on March 16, 1827. Its editors were the Reverend Samuel B.

Cornish, pastor of the African Presbyterian Church in New York and John Russwurm. Russwurm eventually became disenchanted with the lack of opportunity in America and moved to Liberia. Cornish continued publishing the paper under the name of *Rights of All* until 1830.

Education and publishing were not the only fields where Blacks were making their mark. Henry Blair of Maryland received a patent for a corn harvester. Norbert Rillieux of New Orleans was chief engineer of the Louisiana Sugar Refining Company. He revolutionized that industry with the invention of an evaporating pan for the refining of sugar.

Robert Gordon owned a coal yard. Other Blacks were caterers, lumbermen, and grocers. Stephen Smith was probably the wealthiest Black in America during the mid-1800s. He can best be described today as an entrepreneur. His business interests and investments included lumber, railroad cars, and bank stocks.

Nevertheless, despite these achievements, the fundamental condition of Blacks in America was slavery. It was a condition that was becoming increasingly abhorrent to those who advocated its abolition. It was also a condition that was being clung to desperately by those whose very way of life would be unalterably changed should the abolitionists prevail.

(

While Running, Talking, and Active Abolitionists were busy attacking slavery, the fight for abolition shifted to the political arena. Antislavery forces attempted to reject Missouri's request for statehood as a slave state. A compromise was reached in 1820 allowing Maine to enter the Union as a free state and Missouri as a slave state. However, slavery would be restricted in the newly acquired Louisiana Territory. In 1850 another compromise was reached with the admission of California as a free state and the tightening of the Fugitive Slave Law to require local law enforcement officials to assist federal officers in the capture of runaway slaves.

In 1854, under the sponsorship of Senator Stephen Douglas of Illinois, Congress passed the Kansas-Nebraska Act, which had the effect of repealing the Missouri Compromise and opened up lands in the West to slavery. The passage of this act plunged the country into turmoil. Violence erupted in Kansas as pro-slavery and anti-slavery groups fought to settle the land. By the time federal troops restored order more than 200 men and women had been killed.

The politicians of the 1800s were not unlike those of today. Neither major political party, the Whigs nor the Democrats, wanted to take a definitive stand on the issue of slavery. Ultimately anti-slavery members of both parties looked to form a new party dedicated to preventing the further expansion of slavery. On July 6, 1854, in Jackson, Michigan, the Republican Party was formed. How ironic that the Republican Party, which for the past 50 years has been perceived as the party of business interests as opposed to human concerns, has its roots in the tradition of anti-slavery.

The fight for slavery found another battleground. At the Supreme Court the forces of slavery won a great victory in 1857. Dred Scott was a slave. His owner, an Army doctor, had taken him from the slave state of Missouri into the free state of Illinois and then into the free territory of Minnesota. After four years he was returned to Missouri. In 1846, Scott sued for his freedom, claiming that because he had lived in a free area that he was free. The lower courts split in their decisions, and the case went to the Supreme Court. Chief Justice Roger B. Taney, a Southerner, wrote the opinion in favor of Scott's master. Taney reasoned that Blacks "had no rights that the White man had to respect." He further declared that under the Constitution Blacks were not citizens and had no right to sue in court. This decision established the concept that slaves were the property of their masters and that masters could not be deprived of their property by taking it into a free state. Slaves now officially became no better than the master's horse or his plow. Slavery had received the blessing of the highest court in the land, a court where the majority of its occupants were from the South.

53

The political and judicial phases of the abolition question abruptly ended at 4:30AM on April 12, 1861, amidst the sounds and smells of cannon fire crashing into Fort Sumter. Located in the harbor of Charleston, South Carolina, Fort Sumter withstood the battering of Confederate gunners for two days before surrendering. The question of slavery would be settled by war.

«

The beginning of most wars is marked by a surge of public optimism, patriotism, and a sense of invincibility. Unfortunately, the Civil War was no exception. In the North there was a general feeling that the rebellion would put down in short order. There was excitement in the air as blue-coated soldiers marched out of Washington on July 16, 1861 and crossed the Potomac into Virginia in search of the Rebels. It was sunny that day and the local gentry accompanied the soldiers. Armed with the finest wines and picnic baskets, the finely dressed men and women searched for the best place to spread out their blankets and watch the coming battle. Since the war was going to be over shortly, they didn't want to miss the excitement.

The horror of war became a reality to the men dressed in blue as they approached a small stream called Bull Run just outside of Manassas. There a determined Confederate force unleashed a fusillade of cannon and small arms fire that ripped the marching columns apart. Soon the men in blue were in full flight hastening back to Washington before the men in gray could catch and kill them. Now the horror of war became a reality to the gentry as bleeding horses and cursing men streamed past. War was indeed no picnic.

Abraham Lincoln knew that war was no picnic. He did not relish war, but he knew that he could not let the Union of States dissolve. He had been unable to prevent the secession of the Confederate States. Now faced with the realities of the situation, he resolved to focus the mission of the war on the restoration of the Union. He refused to focus the war on the abolition of slavery for a very good reason. Not all slave states had seceded from the Union. It was important for the balance of power to keep those remaining slave states, known as Border States, in the Union. Making the war a crusade for the abolition of slavery would drive them into the Confederacy. To appease the Border States, Lincoln insisted that the objective of the war was the preservation of the Union. In fact, Union Army commanders were instructed to return runaway slaves to their masters whenever possible. They were also instructed to put down any slave revolts in their areas of operations.

Lincoln's desire to keep the issue of slavery out of the war was an impossible wish. As his armies entered the South, runaway slaves and slaves who had been abandoned by their fleeing masters flocked into the Union Army's lines. Their sheer numbers were overwhelming. Although commanders felt obliged to comply with their orders, there was little support among the troops to return slaves to their owners. To further complicate matters, the Union commanders were relying on the slaves to provide information on the location of enemy units and supplies. In addition, the slaves' knowledge of the terrain was of invaluable assistance.

The answer to the problem appeared in the personage of Benjamin Franklin Butler. Butler was a Massachusetts politician who had managed to obtain a commission as a General in the Union Army. He had the unusual ability, perhaps as a result of his political background, always to be at the scene of important events. When he arrived in Virginia and assumed command of Fort Monroe, Butler was soon welcoming slaves into his lines and putting them to work. He simply considered them to be the spoils of war or contraband.[21] With this simple rationalization Butler solved one of the more thorny problems of the war. Lincoln could continue to insist he was not freeing the slaves while at the same time his commanders in the field were freeing slaves under the guise of capturing or confiscating contraband.

❡

With the commencement of hostilities, the United States govern-ment, as in the Revolutionary War, made a conscious decision not to use Black troops. Once again the myth that Blacks were poor fighters pre-vailed. There was also a concern that White troops would refuse to fight alongside Black troops. The initial fervor for the war, however, was soon replaced with caution, concern and even foreboding. The expected early victory did not materialize, and it was soon apparent that the Southern generals outclassed their counterparts in blue.

As the casualties mounted, the reality of war hit home. Mothers began to question why their sons had to die. Men of draft age began to balk at being conscripted. Some even went so far as to pay others to serve in their places. There were protests in the streets. Inevitably the question was asked: "Why can't the Negro fight?" Underlying that ques-tion was a clear understanding in the public's mind that the war was about the abolition of slavery, despite the repeated denials of the President.

Military commanders asked themselves the same question. Now in New Orleans, Ben Butler looked around him and saw thousands of available Black men. From this pool of manpower, he formed the First Louisiana Native Guards in August of 1862. This regiment became the first Black regiment to receive official recognition in the Union Army. It was used to guard the approaches to the city of New Orleans.

The combination of military defeats, the debate over the use of Black troops, and growing public opposition to the war finally brought Lincoln to the realization that something had to be done to focus the country on winning the war. That something was to free the slaves.

Freeing the slaves was not an easy matter. Lincoln couldn't simply announce that he was freeing the slaves. At this point he was losing the war, and any announcement about freeing the slaves would look like an act of desperation and would lack credibility. What he needed was a military victory before he could make the announcement. In Septem-ber of 1862, the Battle of Antietam provided Lincoln his opportunity. Five days after the Union forces prevailed at Antietam Creek, Lincoln

Slaves and Free Blacks served in the Union Army during the Civil War. The above picture shows Company E, 4th U.S. Colored Infantry. *Image courtesy of Documentary Photo Aids.*

issued the Emancipation Proclamation. He announced that he would free all slaves in the states in rebellion on January 1, 1863. The year 1863 would forever be known among Blacks as the *Year of the Jubilee.*

The issuance of the Emancipation Proclamation was one of those poorly kept secrets so characteristic of Washington politics. Anticipation was high in the Black community, but when the actual document was published, the exhilaration of the moment was tempered by disappointment. It freed only those slaves who were residing in the Confederacy. Slaves in the Border States remained slaves. Nevertheless, the Emancipation Proclamation was a dramatic turning point in the war. Blacks were officially welcomed in the military. They now had an equal right to die. By the end of the war, approximately 185,000 Black soldiers fought in the Union Army. The majority, almost 93,000, of them came from Southern states. They served in the combat arms, such as the infantry, artillery, cavalry, and engineers. When it was all over, Abraham

Lincoln, the man who was so reluctant to let Blacks fight, admitted that without the Black soldiers the Union would not have won the war.

The willingness of the Black soldier to fight is remarkable when one considers that the Confederate States had issued a proclamation that Black soldiers would not be treated as prisoners of war. The massacre at Fort Pillow, Tennessee, is stark testimony to this edict. After the fort surrendered, more than 300 Black soldiers, women, and children were murdered by troops under the command of Confederate General Nathan Bedford Forrest. General Forrest later would become one of the founding fathers of the Ku Klux Klan. The Black soldiers' willingness to fight was even more remarkable when you consider the prejudice they faced within their own army. Black soldiers were paid $7.00 per month. Whites received $14.00 per month.

Perhaps the true value of the Emancipation Proclamation was its impact on the Union Army. Until there was a public declaration of Emancipation, only the Confederate soldier knew why he was fighting. He was fighting for his home and his way of life. His clear understanding of his mission translated into tenacity on the battlefield. His White counterpart in blue had no such incentive. He was fighting for the concept of "maintaining the Union." Somehow it wasn't the same and his performance lacked passion. Now, however, he was fighting for a cause. He was freeing slaves. He had a purpose for which he was willing to sacrifice and, if necessary, die.

❆

Once again Black soldiers proved to be courageous and able fighters. While desperately wishing to face the Rebels, they first had to combat prejudice within their own army. The case of the 54th Massachusetts is a particularly good example. Formed at the request of the Governor of Massachusetts, this regiment consisted of Blacks from all walks of life, both slave and free. After completing their training, the regiment was sent south but was restricted to manual labor duties. Except for the persistence of their commanding officer, Colonel Robert Gould Shaw, they probably never would have faced the enemy.

Colonel Shaw was White as were all the officers assigned to the regiment. Shaw had been a Captain at the Battle of Antietam, but he was by no means a professional soldier. The promotion and appointment of this young man from a prominent Massachusetts family as commander of the 54th Regiment exemplified the government's true feelings toward Black soldiers. It was presumed that they would never see combat. Black soldiers were considered inferior as individuals and questionable as fighters. The 54th Massachusetts Regiment would soon dispel these feelings.

The 54th Massachusetts saw its first action at James Island, South Carolina, on July 26,1863. The Regiment is best remembered for its attack on the Confederate stronghold, Fort Wagner, in Charleston, South Carolina. The fort was the key obstacle to be breached in the effort to capture Charleston. It was an excellent fortification located at the mouth of Charleston's harbor. The only suitable avenue of approach required a frontal assault across a narrow beach. The assaulting units would be subjected to withering cannon and rifle fire. Colonel Shaw volunteered the 54th Regiment to lead the assault on Fort Wagner. They attacked in the late afternoon of July 18, 1863. When the sun rose the next morning the beach before Fort Wagner was littered with bodies. The attack had been repulsed and more than half of the men of the 54th would never see another sunset. Fort Wagner was never taken, but the bravery of those Black soldiers has never been forgotten. After this attack there was little hesitation to use Black soldiers in combat.

The attack on Fort Wagner was but one of 39 major battles Black soldiers participated in during the Civil War. As in the Revolutionary War and the War of 1812, the Black American proved his reliability as a soldier. Unfortunately, after the Civil War the stigma of inferiority persisted and the Black soldier would have to prove his worthiness again in World Wars I and II and the Korean War. The Vietnam War was a turning point. Although prejudice was present it was unofficial. From the outset there was no question that Blacks would be given an equal opportunity to die. By the time the Gulf War arrived in the 1990s, the United States military was led into battle by an African-American, General Colin Powell, Chairman of the Joint Chiefs of Staff.

During the Civil War, Black Americans also served in the Union Navy. They were assigned to naval vessels and fought along side their White counterparts. They shared the same hardships, facilities, and quarters. There was no segregation aboard ship if only because of limited space. The famous battle of the ironclads, Monitor and Merrimac, is well known. Less known is the fact that Black sailors were among the crew of the Monitor. All told some 29,000 Blacks served in the Navy. By war's end four had been awarded the Congressional Medal of Honor.

Slaves also played a major role in the Civil War. Large numbers of slaves, upon being freed by Union forces, offered their services as cooks, laborers, nurses, etc. Less known is their contribution as a source of military intelligence. It should be remembered that the Union Army was in unfamiliar territory. This was a distinct advantage for the Confederates who knew the terrain: suitable routes of approach, the availability of bridges, locations of obstacles, the availability of food, etc. The slaves provided this information to Union commanders. Many served as guides. Some, like Harriet Tubman, were spies. Their information and actions changed the course of many a skirmish and hastened the end of the war.

The Civil War ended in the village of Appomatox Court House, Virginia, on April 9, 1865. Slavery was dead, and so it appeared was a way of life for both Blacks and Whites. A period of difficult adjustment was to follow. Slaves were now free men and women. Freedom was no longer a dream; it was a reality.

(

To former slaves, freedom had many faces. Freedom was the ability to sleep, laugh, or do nothing. It was the ability to go wherever they pleased. Blacks by the droves left their plantations. Some simply wandered the countryside searching for what was over the horizon that they had been forced to look at for so long. Others left with a more definite purpose: to find wives, husbands, and children. Many eventually returned, for they had no other place to go or means of making a living.[22]

After the war ended, the South was in a state of general turmoil. The destruction of war had ruined the economy. Homes were destroyed. Local and state governments were unable or unwilling to perform their appropriate functions. Lawlessness prevailed in many localities. Added to this general state of confusion was the return of a defeated and bitter army. Soldiers who had lost on the battlefield returned to find they had lost homes and loved ones as well. It was an explosive situation.

Abraham Lincoln had anticipated these post-war problems prior to the war's end. In March, 1865, Congress had established The Freedman's Bureau. The Bureau helped former slaves start a new life by direct aid. It provided food, shelter, and medical assistance. More importantly, it established schools and provided teachers to give Blacks the education they had been denied in slavery. From 1865-1872, it served as the first federal welfare agency and was an important buffer for the Freedmen from the bitterness permeating the White South. General O. O. Howard, a White officer, headed the Freedman's Bureau. Today, one of the nation's most prestigious, predominately Black educational institutions, Howard University, bears his name.

President Lincoln was prepared to be lenient with the Confederate States. He wanted to ease the return of the Southern states to the Union. For a state to regain full stature in the Union, Lincoln planned to simply require an oath of loyalty to the Constitution and a renouncement of slavery. Unfortunately, his forgiving leadership would be denied the country at the hands of John Wilkes Booth. The assassination of Lincoln eliminated any chance of healing and forgiveness among the former combatants.

❮

The time immediately following the end of the Civil War was a critical point in American history. Although the new President, Andrew Johnson, shared many of Lincoln's beliefs, he lacked the necessary qualities of leadership to guide the country through a smooth transition. The South, fearing the loss of their institutions and way of life, immediately took steps to reinstitute slavery in another form. Soon new local laws were passed that were designed to keep Blacks in bondage. These were the infamous Black Codes.

South Carolina restricted Blacks to the occupation of farming. Mississippi passed a vagrancy law aimed at persons wandering without a job. Persons convicted under this law were fined $50. Those unable to pay could be hired out to any person willing to pay the fine. At the time many newly freed Blacks were wandering the countryside in search of long lost relatives. This law was a thinly disguised attempt to return Black Americans to a condition of slavery. In other states Blacks could be punished for insulting gestures. Black witnesses could not testify against a White person in court, nor could they serve on juries. Some states required Negro travelers to carry passes while others prohibited Negroes from assembling in groups unless there was a White person present. Curfew laws were prevalent. In some cases a Black could be punished for quitting his job, and in others punishment resulted from a wrongful glance.

Violence against Blacks was also running rampart in the South. Armed bands of Whites attacked Blacks at will. Black men who had served with the Union Army were particular targets of White frustration. In May, 1866 in Memphis, Tennessee, in what was officially called a riot, 46 Black men were killed and 75 wounded. Later that year another 40 were killed and nearly 100 wounded in an altercation with police in New Orleans.

❮

The situation in the South was clearly out of control. The fate of

Black America was now placed in the hands of two northern politicians who refused to allow slavery to be reinstituted under another name: Representative Thaddeus Stevens of Pennsylvania and Senator Charles Sumner of Massachusetts.

Politicians in Washington were struggling with the question: "What do we do with the Negro now that he is free?" Lincoln had struggled with this question. He seriously considered deporting the newly emancipated slaves. He gave up on this solution when Ben Butler reported that his study of the matter, based on the reproduction rate of Blacks, showed it to be a physical impossibility. Frederick Douglass believed the answer to the question was to simply leave the freedmen alone. He reasoned that the White folks had already done enough to the Blacks, all of it bad. Douglass argued that, left alone, the Black man would make his way and prosper.

Thaddeus Stevens had another answer. He wanted to break up the former Southern plantations and redistribute the land to the emancipated slaves. Stevens recognized that what the freedmen needed most was the ability to be self-sufficient and provide for themselves. He knew they were skilled farmers. He believed giving them land and the tools to farm the land was the best way to assist them. *Forty Acres and a Mule* became his slogan. Unfortunately, land was never provided.

Although he was unsuccessful in providing forty acres and a mule to the freedmen, Stevens, along with Charles Sumner, was successful in providing protection and economic and political opportunity. Through the efforts of these gentlemen, the Congress passed a law governing the reconstruction of the South. This law divided the South into five military districts with each district being ruled by a Union Army general. The army was to protect the freedmen and restore order. Hopefully, in time, the wounds of the war would heal and Southern Blacks and Whites could live in harmony. Thus began what Lerone Bennett calls *The Ten Improbable Years*, the period from 1867-1877.[23]

With the Union Army firmly in control, the South embarked on a period of ostensible normalcy. At the middle and upper levels of society,

63

Whites and Blacks socialized without apparent discomfort. Black businesses emerged. Blacks went to school, and a Black mother could now dream that her child had a future. Blacks rose to prominence in politics. In Louisiana, when the Governor was impeached, a Black governor, the Honorable P. B. S. Pinchback, briefly replaced him. Blanche K. Bruce was the first Black to serve a full term in the United States Senate. Jefferson P. Long of Georgia was the first Black to be seated in the House of Representatives, serving from 1869-1871. Following the election of Long, 13 more Black Americans, from Southern states, were elected to the House of Representatives between 1871-1876. Blacks were also elected to other high offices. In Arkansas, Mifflin W. Gibbs became the first Black municipal judge in the United States. Jonathan Gibbs, a graduate of Dartmouth College, was elected Secretary of State in Florida. Frederick Cardozo was elected State Treasurer in South Carolina, and in Mississippi John Lynch became the Speaker of the State House of Representatives.

On the other hand, at the lower levels of society things were quite different. The Union Army could not extend its protection into every crook and cranny of the South. Blacks continued to face ostracism at best and violence at its worst. Whites, many of whom were themselves poor and uneducated, feared the new success of their Black counterparts. These fears were exacerbated by racists whose agenda was the reestablishment of White supremacy.

In April, 1867 at the Maxwell House hotel in Nashville, Tennessee, a group of Southern businessmen, former Confederate officers, clergymen and other prominent citizens gathered for the first national meeting of a group soon to be known to the world as the Ku Klux Klan. Historical accounts vary as to the original purpose of the Klan. Some argue that it was originally simply a social organization that later turned to violence. The selection of Nathan Bedford Forrest as its first leader would indicate otherwise. Forrest, a former slave trader, had the distinction of being the Confederate commander who ordered the massacre of defenseless Black men, women, and children at Fort Pillow.

The emergence of the Klan coincided with a campaign among Whites to undermine the political and economic power Blacks had achieved during Reconstruction. It was clear to the Whites that Blacks were skilled in economic and political matters and that given the opportunity they could easily control both the economy and the politics of the South. Whites were determined to prevent this. As long as the Union Army was present, Blacks, who were in the majority, would continue to enjoy economic and political success. Since all efforts to end the army's occupation had been unsuccessful, another way had to be found.

The solution was to control politics at the local level. Such local officials as the city council, zoning board and the sheriff had a more direct impact on the daily lives of the people than did the governor, state legislators, or senators in Washington. Whites reasoned that by controlling the local governments they could control their destiny. Granted, laws passed at the local level could be challenged in court, but the appeal process took time and time was the ally of the White population.

A two-fold plan evolved to ensure White control of local governments. First, terrorist tactics were directed against Blacks to prevent them from voting. Blacks who had attempted to vote were threatened, beaten, or in some cases killed. The second tactic was blatant racism. Businesses that served Blacks suddenly began to lose customers. Whites who associated with or showed sympathy toward Blacks were ostracized. Their children would come home from school reporting that they had been taunted as "nigger lovers." Friendships dissolved. Property was destroyed. And worse, the plan was successful.

The Reconstruction ended as it began, with a political deal. The Presidential election of 1876 between Democrat Samuel Tilden of New York and the former Republican governor of Ohio Rutherford B. Hayes ended in a dispute over electoral votes. To settle the dispute, the Senate appointed an independent commission consisting of eight Republicans and seven Democrats. It was not surprising that the commission's report declared the Republican Hayes the winner, but the commission's report still had to be approved by the Congress, which was controlled by the

Democrats. Seeing an opportunity to remove the Union Army from the South and bring an end to Reconstruction, Southern Democrats struck a deal with the Republican Hayes. They would vote to approve the commission's report if he would agree to remove the army and allow *home rule* in the South. The deal was made. Hayes became President and Black Americans embarked on an 80-year journey of segregation, discrimination, and lynchings.[24]

The Reconstruction left an indelible imprint on America. The divisions between the White South and the Yankee Carpetbagger hardened. Similarly, fear and hatred separated the White southerners from the freedmen in their midst. Blacks, having demonstrated their abilities during the Reconstruction, now became a threat that had to be controlled if not eliminated. Abraham Lincoln's wish for "malice toward none" would not be realized. Rather, it was replaced with stereotypes and resentments that would be passed from generation to generation and continue to plague the United States today.

NOTES

17. W. Augustus Low, ed. and Virgil A. Clift, ed., *Encyclopedia of Black America* (New York: McGraw-Hill Inc., 1981), pp. 279-280

18. Low and Clift, p. 280

19. Bennett, p. 69

20. Low and Clift, p. 787

21. Langston Hughes, Milton Metzger, & Eric Lincoln, *A Pictorial History of Black Americans* (New York: Crown, 1956), p. 165

22. Bennett, pp. 212-213

23. Bennett, p. 216

24. Bennett, pp. 250-252

4

Jim Crow through Thurgood Marshall

As the lines of blue clad men marched north, dark clouds formed in the Southern skies as 1877 came to a close. The South had lost its Peculiar Institution, but it had regained Home Rule. It was now time to re-establish White supremacy and protect a way of life based on the labor of the Black man for the benefit of the White man. In other words, slavery had to be re-instituted under a different name. That name would be Jim Crow.

The origins of the term Jim Crow are somewhat murky. Some say Jim Crow was a slave. Others say he was a soldier. Some claim the term refers to the name of a former slave owner. But all agree that the term became synonymous with a Black man. At first, this Black man was a comic figure made popular in the 1830s by a White vaudeville performer, Thomas Dartmouth Rice. Rice, performing in blackface, would sing and dance on stage to the delight of his audiences. However, by the 1900s there was nothing funny about Jim Crow. It was the symbol of segregation and oppression.

As a slave the Black man posed no threat for he had no power, economic or political. As such, there was no need for Whites to fear Blacks and to some extent the two races shared their environment. During Reconstruction, however, the Black man was given access to economic and political opportunity. Worse yet, he demonstrated considerable ability in both fields of endeavor. As the White Southerners watched Black achievements during Reconstruction, they counted the number of Free Blacks in their midst and realized that Blacks could soon be in a position to control the economic and political affairs of their communities. Now the Black man was a threat and the threat had to be eliminated.

To prevent Blacks from gaining economic and political control of the South, the White state and local governments passed a series of laws designed to restrict Blacks' right to vote, to limit their economic opportunity, to deny them an education, and to keep them in a permanent state of subjugation. For example, Blacks could not be taught by White teachers. There were separate textbooks for White and Black students. In South Carolina it was against the law for White and Black factory workers to look out of the same window. In New Orleans even prostitution was a segregated activity. These were some of the laws that became known as the Jim Crow Laws.

An important goal of Jim Crow was to keep the two races apart. Separating the races prevented friendships from being formed. It prevented understanding through normal contact and discussion. It prevented the development of any sense of empathy between the races. And it created the conditions for perpetuating the concept of White superiority. Therefore, the first and most basic Jim Crow laws were those forbidding *inter-racial eating* and *inter-racial marriage*. Many of these laws remained in force until well into the 1970s. The effects of these laws permeate our national consciousness today.

The act of sharing a meal is in some way an intimate act. When people eat together, they are generally relaxed and receptive to their partner's thoughts and ideas. If the participants are strangers, chances are they will share a common bond before the meal has ended, that they will become friends. Banning inter-racial eating prevented friendships from developing. It prevented familiarity.

This portrait of newly freed slaves shows that although sexual relations between the races was prohibited, some White Southerners were not deterred. *Image courtesy of Documentary Photo Aids.*

If inter-racial eating is an intimate act, inter-racial marriage represented a threat of far greater magnitude. To eliminate this threat, all intimate sexual contact between Whites and Blacks was proscribed. In reality this proscription applied only to contact between White women and Black men. Historically, the White Southern male had never objected to demanding sexual favors of Black women. However, sexual relations between White Women and Black men were not tolerated. Therefore, the White Southern woman became the symbol of the Jim Crow era. Protecting her purity, her virginity, became the holiest mission of the White Southern male. She was not to be insulted or in any way demeaned. The slightest inference that she had been violated was cause for extreme retribution, usually lynching.

Focusing separation of the races on the sanctity of the White woman was a smart tactic. It struck at the basest instincts of the White male: pride, ego, and machismo. When these emotions were aggravated by economic fear or corn whiskey, violence was the usual result. Un-

"Jim Crow" laws gave all Whites police authority over Black Americans. *Image courtesy of Documentary Photo Aids.*

fortunately, as years passed, the concept of the sanctity of the White woman became deeply imbedded in American culture and is no longer restricted to the South. Inter-racial relationships involving White women and Black men are a catalyst for prejudice in many areas of the United States, particularly in areas that are predominantly White.

How the Jim Crow laws came about and how they lasted for so many years is one of the more troubling aspects of any examination of American history. At the time Jim Crow laws first appeared, the 14th and 15th Amendments to the U.S. Constitution were already the law of the land. The 14th Amendment states:

> No State will make or enforce any law that shall abridge the privileges or immunities of citizens of the United States; or shall any State deprive any person of life, liberty, or property without due process of law; nor deny any person within its jurisdiction the equal protection of the laws.

The 15th Amendment states:

> The right of citizens of the United States to vote shall not be denied or abridged by the United States or by any State on account of race, color, or previous condition of servitude.

In addition, in 1875 Congress passed a Civil Rights law that guaranteed equal enjoyment of public facilities, accommodations, transportation, and inns without regard to race, color or previous condition of servitude.

Considering these amendments to the Constitution and the Civil Rights Act of 1875, it would seem impossible for the Southern States to enact legislation denying Blacks their most basic rights and segregating them in every aspect of everyday life. How could it happen? Simply stated, Black America was disenfranchised by two courts: the court of public opinion and the U.S. Supreme Court.[25]

When the Civil War ended, soldiers returned to their homes and the nation looked to the future with a sense of accomplishment. The war had been won. The slaves had been freed. The time of sacrifice was over. It was a time to begin anew, to look to the future. It was also a time of exciting change as Americans focused on the opportunities offered in the newly claimed lands of the American West. There were fortunes to be made and opportunities to be grasped as the country expanded.

It was not a time of particular focus or concern for the plight of the Black American. He was free. He, too, could take advantage of the new opportunities. The court of public opinion in America essentially said, "You are on your own!" What was overlooked was that until now it had

71

been against the law for Blacks to become educated. Many could not read. Most had no money. Few had the skills to take advantage of the opportunity of Westward expansion. Fewer still had the ability to demand the rights so eloquently written in the Constitution and in the Civil Rights Act.

Public opinion in Europe, particularly in England, had been of enormous assistance to the Abolitionist Movement in the United States. Slavery had been outlawed in many European countries and was generally abhorred by the common man. Once the American slaves gained their freedom, Europeans also focused their attention on other matters. It was the time of the Industrial Revolution. The new machines of mass production had voracious appetites that required ever-increasing raw materials. Europe looked to Africa and colonies to meet these needs. The Age of Imperialism had begun. European concern for the American Negro was no longer a topic of drawing room discussions.

☾

Black America could probably have withstood the loss of favorable national and international public opinion had it not been for the decisions rendered by the United States Supreme Court. The Court, whose members were granted life terms of office to free them from the pressures of partisan politics, succumbed to the political winds of the times. In decision after decision the Court undermined the rights of Black Americans and provided the vehicle for an ever-increasing passage of Jim Crow laws. In the Slaughterhouse Case of 1873, the Court decided that state and national citizenship are separate and distinct. It further explained that the 14th Amendment applied only to laws affecting national citizenship. Since most Jim Crow laws were state laws and affected only state citizenship the impact of the 14th Amendment was virtually negated. In 1883 the Court further restricted the impact of the 14th Amendment. In the case of the United States v. Harris, 20 members of a lynch mob were to be tried under the Ku Klux Klan Act of

A *separate but equal* classroom. *Image courtesy of Documentary Photo Aids.*

1871. In this case the accused had beaten four Black prisoners. One of the prisoners died as a result of his wounds. The Court ruled that the 14th Amendment applied only to State action and not to the actions of individuals. The Court required the accused to be tried in a State Court. Thus began a pattern of violence directed at Black Americans followed by a series of acquittals by all White juries.

The Supreme Court did not forget the 15th Amendment in its deliberations. In the case of the *United States v. Reese* in 1876, the Court reasoned that the 15th Amendment did not guarantee the right to vote, but rather simply prohibited federal and state governments from excluding persons from voting based on race, color, or previous condition of servitude. By splitting hairs and manipulating semantics, the Supreme Court opened the door to grandfather clauses, poll taxes, property tests, and literacy tests that prevented Blacks from voting until 1965 when President Lyndon Johnson signed the Voting Rights Act.

Finally in 1883 the Supreme Court struck down the Civil Rights Act of 1875. The Court reasoned that this law was unconstitutional on the grounds that it violated the 14th Amendment. It argued that private actions, as envisioned in the Civil Rights Act of 1875, were not addressed by the Constitution. To further justify its position, the Court stated that the Civil Rights Act of 1875 violated the 13th Amendment as well. It claimed the 13th Amendment was only intended to end slavery, not discrimination.

《

The decisions of the Supreme Court restricting the interpretations of the 14th and 15th Amendment and its subsequent overturning of the Civil Rights Act of 1875 were like the crescendo in a musical composition. With each stanza the music becomes more forceful until it peaks with a thunderous clap, like the cannons of the "1812 Overture." The cannon for the Supreme Court's composition on the civil rights of Black Americans was its *Plessy v. Ferguson* decision. In the Plessy case the Supreme Court had ruled that states had the authority to require separate but equal facilities for Blacks and Whites. It legitimatized separation of the races in all aspects of life for the next 58 years. In reality, it legitimatized the concept of separate and unequal. Only Justice John Marshall Harlan foresaw problems. In his dissent of the Plessy decision, Harlan argued that the decision would lead to increased aggression against Blacks and the birth of a caste system based on a concept of inferiority. At the dawn of the twenty-first century, Justice Harlan's words continue to haunt the American landscape.

Armed with the Supreme Court's Plessey decision, the White south embarked on passage of a myriad of laws to keep the races segregated and to prevent Blacks from gaining economic and political power. The most important of these laws were designed to prevent Blacks from voting, thus negating the fact that Blacks were in the majority in many states. The laws were very effective. In Louisiana, within two years of enactment, the number of registered Black voters went from 130,000 to 5,000. By 1900 there were only 3,000 registered Black voters in Alabama. The laws included literacy tests, property tests, and poll taxes.

Literacy tests required that a person be able to read in order to vote. During slavery it was against the law to teach a slave to read. Consequently, many adult Black Americans were unable to read and therefore couldn't vote. Property tests required that for a person to vote he or she must show evidence of owning property. Most Blacks at the time were employed as tenant farmers and did not own property. Finally, voters were required to pay a poll tax before receiving a ballot. The tax in itself was not particularly high, a few dollars at most. However, for the Black American with a family to feed and no money, the tax achieved its intended purpose. Blacks couldn't afford to vote.

If humor can be found in these travesties, it was that poor, uneducated Whites were also affected by these laws. They too were unable to vote and they objected. Their objections, however, were heard and resolved by the enactment of the *grandfather clause*. Grandfather clauses excused any person, whose ancestors who were eligible to vote prior to 1866, from the requirements of the literacy tests, property tests, and poll taxes. This effectively allowed all Whites to vote. Since no Black was allowed to vote prior to 1866, the grandfather clauses were not applicable to them.

There remained one category of poor, uneducated White still to be accounted for. Immigrant Whites who arrived in the United States after the Civil War were not covered by the grandfather clauses so a special clause, the *understanding clause*, was enacted to allow them to vote. If a person could not read or write but could demonstrate an ability to understand the Constitution, then he could vote. Oddly, no Whites failed this test, but Blacks never were capable of understanding sufficiently to receive a ballot.

❦

As early as 1879, Blacks in the South realized that their situation would only get worse, that their children would continue to face economic peonage, White violence, and lack of educational opportunity. In what became known as the Exodus of 1879, approximately 50,000 Blacks fled to the North. More would have left, but many were prevented by Whites who needed to keep a cheap and powerless labor force. With the Army gone, with public opinion indifferent to their plight, and with the Supreme Court consistently ruling against them, the Blacks who remained in the South were subjected to increasing violence at the hands of their White neighbors.

Lynching, the indiscriminate killing of Blacks, became a public sport. Although technically illegal, lynchings were nevertheless condoned and even advertised in local newspapers as upcoming events. From 1890-1900 over twelve hundred Blacks were killed without the benefit of a trial. It didn't matter if they were guilty. To lose their lives, they simply had to be accused or be in the wrong place. Some lynchings were the result of mob unrest over a real or imagined rape. Some were the result of a few drunks looking for excitement. Some were deliberate attempts to terrorize the Black community for no reason other than intimidation. Other lynchings were for such crimes as testifying against a White in court, disputing the price of a product, or being disrespectful to Whites by failing to say "Mister." And lynching was not an act that was constrained by gender. In 1919, Mary Turner was lynched in Valdosta, Georgia. Although pregnant Mary was tied to a tree doused with gasoline and burned. To complete their gruesome work, Mary's killers cut open her stomach and killed her unborn child.[26]

Another notorious means of controlling Blacks was the Chain Gang. The Chain Gang consisted of Black prisoners who were forced to work at hard labor. Sometimes they were chained together. Manacles were placed on the ankles and a chain run through, connecting each prisoner but allowing sufficient slack for the man or woman to work. In other instances prisoners would be chained individually to a heavy cement ball that would drag along behind them. In either case the conditions on the Chain Gang were deplorable, and the workers were constantly subject to a whipping at the whim of their guards.

A lynching in the United States. Lynching is most often associated with the practice of hanging. However, in 1999 James Byrd was lynched in Texas when three white supremacists chained him to the back of their truck and dragged him at high speeds until he was decapitated. *Image courtesy of Documentary Photo Aids.*

The true purpose of the Chain Gang was to control recalcitrant Blacks. The goal was to break the individual's spirit in the hope that he would no longer be a problem. An additional goal was to set an example for others who might wish to protest their station in life. Blacks, particularly young males who showed qualities of leadership, were arrested on the slightest pretext, convicted, and sent to work. They lived in squalid conditions, working from dawn to dusk. By the time a prisoner's sentence was completed, the goal was often achieved. Remarkably, many survived this experience with their spirit in tact.

❨

During the years of Reconstruction Black Americans realized achievements in business, education, and politics. The years that followed Reconstruction were far less satisfactory. Many Blacks were forced to return to the their old plantations as tenant farmers or sharecroppers, working in a system that guaranteed poverty. Black craftsmen whose skills were in demand were excluded from unions in both the North and the South. When they could find work, it was generally for lower wages. Often the only work they could find was as strike breakers, thus insuring the enmity of their White counterparts.

The educational achievements of the Reconstruction period were now slowed as separate but equal school systems received unequal appropriations from local and state governments. South Carolina is a prime example. In 1915 it spent $13.98 to educate a White child and $2.57 for a Black child. Political achievements waned as more Blacks lost the right to vote.

It was in the context of this environment that the seeds of a titanic struggle were planted. The goal was the social, political and economic advancement of Black Americans. How to achieve the goal was at the center of the struggle. It became a struggle of two strong egos housed in the bodies of Booker T. Washington and W. E. B. Du Bois.

☾

Booker Taliaferro Washington was born on a Virginia plantation. The product of a White planter and a colored slave, Washington was never sure of the exact date of his birth. Others have established it as April 15, 1856. When the Civil War ended, Washington's family settled in Malden, West Virginia. Encouraged by his mother to strive for a better life, Washington recognized the importance of an education. However, he had little opportunity to go to school and spent most of his boyhood working in the coal mines. Eventually he obtained a position as a house-boy in the home of General Lewis Ruffner, one of the more distinguished citizens in Malden. He lived with the Ruffners for approximately two years. General Ruffner's wife, a Vermont Yankee, took an interest in young Booker. She was very strict in the management of her household and taught Booker the importance of cleanliness, order, and efficiency in one's daily activities. She also encouraged his efforts to obtain an education and made certain that he had time to attend classes. Washington later looked back on his time with Mrs. Ruffner as one of the most important educational experiences of his life.

While he was working in the mines, Washington learned of a school for Negroes in Hampton, Virginia, some 500 miles away. He left Malden to enroll in Hampton Institute in the fall of 1872. He arrived at Hampton with 50 cents in his pocket. He was eager to begin his studies but first had to be admitted to the school.

Fate has a strange way of changing the course of history. When Washington approached the head teacher to request admission to Hampton, he was, not surprisingly, ignored. His appearance after so long a trip was not exactly inspiring, and for a moment it appeared that he might not be admitted. Eventually, the teacher pointed to a room and instructed Washington to clean it. Now the lessons he had learned from Mrs. Ruffner served him well. Never had a room been cleaned so thoroughly, and when the head teacher inspected his work, she admitted him without further hesitation.[27] Washington now embarked on a journey that would leave an indelible imprint on Black America and bring him fame, riches, and ridicule.

The Director of Hampton Institute was General Samuel C. Armstrong. Armstrong had commanded colored troops during the Civil War and believed that industrial education was the key that would unlock the door of success for Black Americans. He believed that Black America should adapt to the realities of Jim Crow, forsake for the moment the politics of protest, and focus instead on economic advancement. As a student and later as a member of the Hampton faculty, Washington greatly admired General Armstrong. Later, as President of Tuskegee Institute, Washington would adopt the philosophy of industrial education and political accommodation as his own.

In 1881 Booker T. Washington assumed the presidency of a new school for Black Americans in Tuskegee, Alabama. For the next 34 years the name of Washington and his institute at Tuskegee were synonymous. He nurtured and developed the school through his personal diligence, the hard work of his students, and the philanthropy of White benefactors such as Andrew Carnegie. Tuskegee became a model for vocational education, a shining example of Black achievement. It also became a powerful base from which Washington influenced American politics. In fact, by the early 1900s, it was generally conceded that no politician, Black or White, would make a major decision or appointment that affected the American Negro without first consulting with Washington.

Washington was able to acquire political power for a variety of reasons. He was generally admired for his success at Tuskegee. The Black community appreciated his efforts and recognized that vocational education provided an opportunity for a better life. As a result, he received favorable approval from most of the Black press. His relations with the White community were even better. He adopted a policy of accommodation with Jim Crow. He counseled Blacks not to fight the policies of segregation. He believed that economic achievement and economic independence were the keys for opening the door of equal rights to Black

Americans. He made Whites comfortable. For this Washington and Tuskegee were the benefactors of substantial financial contributions. In fact, Andrew Carnegie specified in his gift to Tuskegee that a portion of the money be designated for the personal use of Washington.[28]

Washington was a complex individual full of contradictions. While counseling Blacks to accept segregation, he refused to obey Jim Crow laws and would ride first class when traveling by train. In his dealings with White Southerners, he could be most submissive, yet he socialized and was accepted in the highest circles of White society, dining at the White House with President Theodore Roosevelt. And while he counseled Black Americans to forget about politics, he in turn possessed tremendous political power.

In September 1895, Washington was invited to speak before the Cotton States Exposition in Atlanta, Georgia. He delivered a speech on race relations. Standing before the predominantly White audience, he talked about fear being the cause of misunderstanding. He spoke of a boat that was lost at sea and without water. The sailors were afraid to drink what they believed to be salt water. Sighting another boat on the horizon, the lost sailors sent a signal requesting water. The reply instructed them to cast down their buckets where they were. Reluctantly the sailors cast their buckets over the side and to their amazement drew in fresh water. Unknown to them, they had entered the mouth of the Amazon River. When they overcame their fear and took a chance they found there was no longer a problem. Washington told his audience to "cast down their buckets" as well. If Blacks and Whites would stay where they were and take a chance, they could live together in harmony. He raised his hand in a clenched fist proclaiming that on matters of mutual interest the Black and White races could come together and act as one. Then, opening his hand and separating his fingers, he said that on other matters, not of mutual concern, the races could act as separately as his spread fingers. In what became known as the *Atlanta Compromise*, Washington in effect endorsed the concept of separate but equal that the U. S. Supreme Court would adopt in *Plessy v. Ferguson* the following May. Reaction to Washington's Atlanta Compromise speech was swift. His stunned White audience loved it and engulfed him with their cheers. There were no cheers from the few Blacks in the audience, nor were there cheers from the Black community at large. In the months that followed, critics of Washington emerged to attack him.

Washington did not adopt his policy of accommodation nor his focus on vocational education in a vacuum. From 1890 through the end of 1893 over 500 Black Americans had been lynched at the hands of Whites. Washington wanted to stop this carnage and believed that by living together and casting down their buckets, the two races would learn to accept each other and understand one another. Then, he hoped, the lynching would stop. He also knew that the future of his people rested on a good education and that White people would have to provide the money. Washington's endorsement of "separate but equal" was his way of opening the doors to White support of Black education. Unfortunately, all his White audience heard was the word *separate.* Equality was not a consideration. By the end of 1895, there had been another 113 lynchings. Money for Black education was not forthcoming.

Washington's critics condemned his policy of accommodation. Among them were John Hope, the president of Atlanta Baptist College; Charles Chestnut, a celebrated novelist; and Monroe Trotter, the editor of *The Boston Guardian.* These men recoiled at the idea that they had to wait for equality. So too did Dr. W. E. B. Du Bois, the man who would become Washington's most severe critic and personal nemesis.

❰

William Edward Burghart Du Bois was born in 1868 in the western Massachusetts town of Great Barrington. His formative years were spent in this relatively peaceful New England town free from racial strife. At 16 he graduated from high school and went south to attend Fisk University, an all Black school in Nashville, Tennessee. In his freshman year he came face to face with Jim Crow. Lynchings were a reality

W. E. B. Du Bois, 1868-1963. *Image courtesy of Documentary Photo Aids.*

of life in Tennessee, and many of his classmates armed themselves when leaving the campus. While at Fisk he also encountered the irrational hate generated by Jim Crow. Du Bois recalled, in a memoir entitled *Darkwater*, an occasion when he accidentally bumped into a White woman. In a gesture of apology, Du Bois doffed his cap. His gesture was greeted by an angry explosion of vindictive expletives. It was an experience he long remembered, and he claimed to never again have raised his hat to a Southern White woman.

Du Bois had another significant experience at Fisk. For the first time he came in close contact with large numbers of African Americans whose upbringing had been considerably different from his own. Contact with his classmates brought a new perspective to his outlook on life. A more powerful and lasting impression, however, came as the result of his summer work as a teacher in the local countryside. Here he encountered poverty, ignorance, and lost opportunity that would provide the foundation for his most celebrated book *The Souls of Black Folk.*

In 1888 Du Bois entered Harvard University and by 1895, as Booker T. Washington was preparing to make his Atlanta Compromise, Du Bois became the first Black American to receive the degree of Ph.D. from that prestigious institution. Following graduation he briefly accepted positions at Wilberforce University and the University of Pennsylvania. He then accepted a position at Atlanta University. As chairman of the Department of History and Economics he gained national and international recognition.

W. E. B. Du Bois refused to accept that the Negro was an inferior race. He refused to accept that Negroes were to be denied the full rights of citizenship. He refused to accept that the White man could heap indignities on Blacks with impunity. He refused to accept that the laws were not applied equally to all men. In short, he believed that all men were equal and should be so treated. Believing these things invariably brought Du Bois into conflict with the most prominent Black leader of the times, Booker T. Washington.

The breach between Washington and Du Bois was inevitable. The two men came from starkly different backgrounds and experiences. Washington had been born a slave. He had struggled to get his education. When Washington was a boy, it had been illegal to teach a slave to read. As a mature man he looked out on a society that was struggling just to exist. He believed he could end the suffering of his people by teaching them life sustaining skills. On the other hand, Du Bois had grown up among White people. He was educated at the best schools. Although he had encountered racism as a student at Fisk, he never lived a life of degradation. His was the experience of an academician.

Unlike Washington, Du Bois believed that Jim Crow should be attacked at its roots and that Black Americans should demand and immediately receive the full rights of citizenship. He believed Blacks should have equal access to education as well. Blacks had the right to be doctors, lawyers, and bankers. They had the right to prepare themselves for whatever profession they wished to enter.

He was, however, a realist. He recognized that not all Blacks were ready to achieve these goals. Therefore, he suggested that the best and the brightest, the top ten percent of Black youths be identified and given the opportunity to a full education. From this group he expected the future leaders of Black America would emerge. This idea would become known as *The Talented Tenth*.[29] Clearly Du Bois rejected any concept of accommodation to Jim Crow. He rejected limiting educational opportunity to vocational skills. To do so, he believed, would predetermine Black Americans to second class citizenship.

Du Bois was not alone in these beliefs. Among those who supported Du Bois were Monroe Trotter, editor of the *Boston Guardian*; Clement

Morgan, Trotter's Harvard classmate; and Harry Clay Smith, editor of the *Cleveland Gazette*. These men and others like them were alarmed at the accommodating policies of Booker T. Washington and the limiting affects of his emphasis on vocational education. Perhaps of greater concern was the impact of Washington on White America. Washington had been embraced by influential Whites as a savior. He had powerful financial support from men like Andrew Carnegie. He was, in fact, the most powerful Negro in America, and in their view he must be stopped.

On July 10, 1905, at the invitation of W. E. B. Du Bois, 29 Black leaders gathered at Fort Erie, Ontario to outline a plan to demand full citizenship rights for the American Negro. It is somewhat ironic that because of racial prejudice in Buffalo, New York, this first effort to organize for American civil rights was held on Canadian soil. The conference focused on enforcement of the 14th and 15th Amendments to the U. S. Constitution, integration of public facilities, improved educational facilities, and the right of free men everywhere to assemble freely and speak their minds. Of particular concern was the equal application of the laws by the police and the courts to all citizens. The conference would become known to the world as the Niagara Movement. However, despite its imposing name and the follow-up meetings in Harper's Ferry, Boston and other places, the Niagara Movement never truly became an effective agent for change. Its true historical significance is that it represents the first attempt to organize Black Americans into a national organization for civil rights. From this humble beginning would eventually emerge the powerful *National Association for the Advancement of Colored People* (NAACP).

While the Niagara Movement struggled, two events occurred that thrust the plight of the American Negro onto the front pages of American newspapers and into the conscience of White America. In September, 1906, a White mob, reinforced by the local police, viciously attacked the Black community of Atlanta. In the aftermath of the riot, known as *The Atlanta Massacre*, it became clear that the cause was not, as originally claimed, retribution for assaults by Black men on White women. Rather, it was the result of White resentment and fear of Blacks entering the workforce and establishing their rightful place in society. Shocking as it was, the impact of that massacre was lessened by the fact that it had occurred in a Southern city. However, in August 1908, a White mob seeking revenge for an alleged rape of a White woman by a Black man indiscriminately attacked defenseless Blacks in Springfield, Illinois. Six people were shot, two were lynched, and thousands fled their homes. *The Springfield Massacre* was a shock that could not be avoided or rationalized. Springfield, Illinois was the home of Abraham Lincoln. It was a northern city. The fierceness of that attack on the Black community was clear evidence of a far deeper national problem.

The Atlanta and Springfield Massacres left no doubt that Black Americans needed protection. Blacks and Whites alike saw the need for an organization that could effectively advance the cause of Black America, an organization that was financially strong, an organization that could have a direct impact on the political process. On May 30,1909, three hundred Americans gathered in New York City and created that organization, *The National Association for the Advancement of Colored People* (NAACP). At a second conference in May 1910, a permanent organization was established for the NAACP. Its first president was Moorefield Storey, a Boston lawyer. Ironically, Mr. Storey was White, as were all other members of the Board of Directors with the exception of W. E. B. Du Bois. Du Bois was appointed to the position of Director of Research and Publicity. In time the leadership of the NAACP was assumed by Black Americans, and the organization fulfilled the dream of its organizers. It became the foundation for the Civil Rights Movement and the battles and victories of the 1940s, 1950s, and 1960s.

A month after the establishment of the NAACP, on July 4th, 1910, Jack Johnson, the Black heavyweight boxing champion, defended his crown against the Great White Hope, Jim Jeffries. This was a fight packed with emotion. Johnson had won the title in 1908, the first Black to do so. He was a brash and arrogant man who loved to be seen in public with a White woman on his arm. Johnson was an unsubtle threat to the very concept of White superiority. White America couldn't wait for him to get a good old-fashioned whipping at the hands of Jeffries. When Johnson beat Jeffries, riots broke out across the country. Although Johnson had proved, beyond any doubt, that the Black man was the equal of any White, it was a lesson with a bloody price tag.

❦

The beginning of the 1900s is called the Progressive Era in most U. S. History books.[30] It was a time when the plight of the working man and the poor were the focus of great attention. Investigative reporters and journalists known as *Muckrakers* exposed corruption and crime in government and business. Upton Sinclair wrote *The Jungle*, a blistering expose of the meat packing industry. Lincoln Steffens exposed government corruption in *The Shame of the Cities*. It was a time when women were clamoring for the right to vote. It was a time when the Australian ballot was introduced into the election process.

The leading figure of the Progressive Movement was President Theodore Roosevelt. Roosevelt was a colorful, energetic, earnest individual. As President he used these qualities to improve the lives of many Americans. Prior to assuming office, he had had a varied career ranging from cowboy to Governor of New York. It was, however, his much-publicized charge up San Juan Hill in the Spanish-American War that thrust him into national prominence. This event depicting Roosevelt as the dashing commander of a cavalry unit called the Rough Riders was the subject of newspaper reports across the country. Eventually it became a symbol of daring and bravery that led Roosevelt to the White House.

A closer look at the event known as the charge up San Juan Hill is a revealing insight into the character of Roosevelt. Although depicted as a cavalry charge, the attack actually took place on foot. The Rough Riders' horses had been left behind when the unit went to Cuba. Then, too, the attack took place on Kettle Hill, not San Juan Hill.[31] Having reached the summit of the hill, Roosevelt and his men were immediately subjected to a counter attack by Spanish forces and were quickly surrounded. At that point the Ninth and Tenth Cavalry, Negro units, came to the rescue.

After the battle Roosevelt acknowledged his gratitude and respect for the Negro troops. Unfortunately, gratitude and respect are fleeting emotions. As president, Roosevelt did little to advance the cause of Black Americans. In 1901 he invited Booker T. Washington to dine at the White House. Since White reaction to the invitation was decidedly negative, Roosevelt never entertained another Black while in office.

Nonetheless, the Black community generally admired him until a crisis erupted in Brownsville, Texas, in August, 1906. Black troops of the First Battalion 25th Infantry Regiment were accused of shooting up the town, killing a White bartender and wounding a policeman. After a preliminary investigation and without the benefit of a trial, Roosevelt signed an order discharging 167 Black soldiers. The men received less than honorable discharges, and those who were eligible lost their pensions.[32] Roosevelt's actions in this case are hard to justify, especially coming from a man who owed his life to Black soldiers and who proudly called his administration *The Square Deal.*

(

The Progressive Years saw no reduction in lynchings. Records kept at Tuskegee list 885 lynchings between 1900-1909. Nor were these years progressive for the Black workingman. After the Civil War, industry once again looked to expand and markets in the South offered new opportunity for profits. The good jobs that accompanied the new industries were not available to Blacks. By 1900, only 4% of the Negroes in the South were employed in skilled industries. It wasn't much different in the North where unions excluded Black membership. If a Black could get a job at all, it was as an unskilled laborer at the lowest level of pay.

There is an ironic twist to the exclusion policies of the major unions. Unions at the turn of the century were struggling for acceptance and even for survival. The tycoons of business looked upon the unions with scorn, as did the Federal Government. The one effective weapon available to the unions in their quest for higher wages and better working conditions was the strike. By excluding Blacks from membership, the unions negated their only advantage. When the unions went on strike, the owners simply hired Black workers as strike breakers. The Blacks, having no other options, took the work to put food on their tables. Yet even in the face of this reality, the unions continued their exclusionary policies. Eventually, unions such as the American Federation of Labor reached out to Blacks. But even then it was only a partial gesture as they formed separate, segregated locals. From this practice grew a series of separate unions in a variety of disciplines ranging from painters to dock workers.[33]

Despite these problems Black America was on the move. By 1913, Black Americans owned over 500,000 homes; more than 70% of the Black population was literate; over one million Black children were attending public schools; and Blacks had entered the fields of medicine, dentistry, law, and nursing.[34] They would soon be on the move physically as well. In April 1913, Henry Ford came up with his idea of the assembly line from which came an inexpensive automobile known as the "Model T." Ford's idea was to provide affordable transportation for the American people. By so doing, he provided Black Americans with the means to escape the South and to begin anew somewhere else. Another generation of Blacks left the South. They settled in the cities of the North, East, and West. The face of America changed forever.

As Blacks migrated to new parts of the country, they brought with them a distinctive culture: a mixture of their African past, the trials of slavery, and the problems of the present. It was a culture that found expression in the music of African rhythms and the soulful sounds of slave row. But the bedrock of this culture was the Black church. Through the church, traditions were passed on to succeeding generations. The church provided a safe haven from White power. The degradation of segregation with its implications of inferiority was a world away when worshipping or attending a church social event. Its ministers were articulate, educated men who were trusted and looked to for advice.

The church served as a spawning ground for political and economic activity. It was the centerpiece of Black society. As we view the history of Black America, it is not surprising that the leaders were and are men of the cloth: the Reverend Richard Allen, the Reverend Absalom Jones, the Reverend James Healey, the Reverend Adam Clayton Powell, the Reverend Martin Luther King, the Reverend Jesse Jackson, the Reverend Andrew Young, the Reverend Al Sharpton.

The migration of Blacks changed the face of our great cities as well. In the 1890s, Blacks in New York were scattered throughout the city. Many Blacks, working as domestics, lived near their rich employers. Harlem was a predominantly White neighborhood. However, in 1903, Blacks began to move into apartment buildings in the area of 134th Street. As the Black population increased, Whites began to move out. Before long Harlem was a completely Black community.

Two results of historical significance came from the Harlem experience. First, Harlem developed into the center of Black culture famous for its particular contributions to music and literature. Claude Mckay, James Weldon Johnson, and Langston Hughes found expression for their poems and novels among the sounds and smells of Harlem. Hall Johnson formed a group of young Harlem singers to perform Negro folk songs.[35] This group went on to perform in concerts and films as The Hall Johnson Choir. Duke Ellington, his band, and his jazz made Harlem the music capital of New York for Whites and Blacks alike in the 1920s.

The second historical legacy of the birth of Harlem was not as bright. From it came the tradition of "Black fright, White flight." The exodus of Whites from Harlem began an unfortunate pattern that continues in our country as we begin the twenty-first century. When Blacks move into an area, Whites leave. As in the case of Harlem, if only a few Blacks move in, Whites do not react. However, as numbers increase ever so slightly, Whites begin to leave. From this paradox myths evolved that, though untrue, have become accepted as fact. Some examples of false myths include the following: as the number of Blacks increase, property values decrease; as the number of Blacks increase, crime rates increase; and as the number of Blacks increase, educational standards decrease.

☾

In the election of 1912, Woodrow Wilson knew he would need the Black vote. He met with Black leaders and promised that he would be president of all the people, that his administration would veto legislation that was hostile to African Americans, and that his distribution of political patronage would be colorblind.[36] After the disappointing racial policies of Teddy Roosevelt's Square Deal, Black Americans looked hopefully to Woodrow Wilson's *New Freedom* and supported him at the polls. After the election their hopes were dashed when in 1913, the administration of Woodrow Wilson authorized the segregation of federal offices in Washington, D.C.

Black hopes were not the only ones dashed by Woodrow Wilson. In November 1916, Wilson was re-elected to a second term, using the slogan "he kept us out of war." On April 2, 1917, he abandoned that pledge and asked the Congress to declare war on Germany and its allies in order to make the world safe for democracy. The United States entered World War I with patriotic fervor. Soon it seemed the whole country was singing that the Yanks were coming *Over There.*

As the United States embarked on its crusade to make the world safe for democracy, it was blind to the contradiction that democracy was not safe at home. In the year before we entered the war, 54 Black Americans were lynched. In the year that the United States committed itself to stop the killing in Europe, 38 Black Americans were lynched. On July 28, 1917, ten thousand Black Americans gathered in New York City to protest the lynchings and continuous discrimination directed at the Black community. Dressed in white they silently marched down Fifth

Avenue carrying a banner that read "Mr. President, Why Not Make America Safe for Democracy?" In 1918, sixty-four Black Americans were lynched. When the war ended in 1919 and the world was now "safe for democracy," 83 Black Americans were lynched.[37]

☾

Shortly after the United States' entry into World War I, in an action reminiscent of George Washington's prohibition of Black participation in the Revolutionary War, the War Department stopped accepting Negro volunteers into the services. Prior to that no Blacks were allowed in the Coast Guard, the Marines or the fledgling Army Air Force. Later, when the draft was implemented, Blacks were allowed, but not accepted.

The case of Lieutenant Charles Young is a tragic example of America's reluctance to accept Black Americans or to judge them, except on the basis of color.[38] Young was a West Point graduate. While commanding a squadron of the 10th Cavalry in Mexico, he had distinguished himself in combat against the forces of Pancho Villa at Aguascalientes and again at Santa Cruz de Villegas. When the Army expanded for war, Young's career should have been in a position to rise rapidly. Instead his career was cut short by the forces of racial prejudice and political expediency. On July 30, 1917, Charles Young was promoted to Colonel and, over the objections of the medical officers who had examined him, was medically retired from active duty. As a demonstration of his physical stamina and his objection to having been retired, he rode from Ohio to Washington, D.C., on horseback. Along the way Black supporters repeatedly cheered him, but to no avail. He was not allowed to serve his country against the enemy in Europe. Other Blacks, however, did fight in Europe. At times it was uncertain who their enemy was, Germany or the United States Army.

Black America was faced with a difficult decision. Blacks had shed their blood in every American war. Some were questioning for what purpose. Lynchings still occurred with regularity, and Jim Crow was the law of the land. Why then should they sacrifice their sons for a distant war in Europe? It took the pen of W. E. B. Du Bois to answer that question. As the editor of the NAACP's newspaper, *The Crisis,* Du Bois had access to the thoughts of Black Americans across the country. In a July 1918 editorial, *Close Ranks,* he asked his readership to "forget our special grievances and close ranks shoulder to shoulder with our White fellow citizens and the allied nations that are fighting for democracy." Coming from Du Bois the message had a forceful impact.

Du Bois was known for his uncompromising stance on equality for Blacks. He was at the forefront of the struggle for full educational opportunity. He abhorred Jim Crow and rejected accommodation. Yet here he was arguing for Black Americans to put aside differences and fight for their country while other Black leaders were willing to boycott the war. His motivation for writing this editorial was his understanding that Black Americans had little choice but to take part in the war. Should they refuse, Whites would forever hold that as an excuse to deny them the rights of full citizenship. However, if they did their duty, they would be in a strong position to argue for their rights once the war was over. It was a compelling argument, but unfortunately unrealistic.

❦

The Black experience in World War I can be described in two words: brave and brutal. Once again Black Americans acquitted themselves heroically under fire. Sergeant Henry Johnson became the first American soldier to win the French *Croix de Guerre* for bravery. Johnson and another Black soldier, Needham Roberts, were manning a two-man outpost when approximately 20 German soldiers attacked them. Johnson and Roberts successfully defended their outpost, killing four of the Germans and wounding several others. At one point in the battle, the Germans captured Roberts. Johnson, now out of ammunition, attacked the Germans using his rifle as a club. When the battle ended, both men were decorated for bravery.

At about the same time a White soldier who had been a conscientious objector was also decorated for bravery in action. Sergeant Alvin York, a Quaker from Kentucky, had single handedly destroyed several German machine gun nests and captured a large body of enemy troops. For his efforts he was awarded the Congressional Medal of Honor, the United States equivalent of the *Croix de Guerre.* York became the darling of the press. His exploits were the subject of a Hollywood movie. His name was known and admired by a generation of White Americans who never heard of Henry Johnson or Needham Roberts.

Johnson and Roberts were members of the 369th Infantry Regiment. The Regiment was from New York City and had formerly been a National Guard unit known as the Harlem Hell Fighters. In France it distinguished itself. It was the first American unit to cross the Rhine River, and though it was under fire for 191 days, the longest sustained period of combat by any American unit in World War I, it never lost a man to capture.

The 369th had not been allowed to cross the Atlantic with the other elements of the American Expeditionary Force, also known as the Rainbow Division. The Rainbow Division had received its name from the wide variety of National Guard units that had been joined together to form the division. The 369th was excluded. It was later explained that Black is not a color of the Rainbow.

The 369th Regiment arrived at Brest, France in December 1917. It was assigned to the French Army because of the French's desperate need for manpower and because of the Americans' distaste for having Black troops among them. The 369th for all purposes became a French unit. Its weapons and uniforms were French and it was listed in the French Order of Battle. Accordingly, its commander Colonel William Hayward called his unit The Lost Children or, in French, "*Les Enfants Perdus.*"[39]

Discrimination based on color was not prevalent in the French culture. The French people welcomed the 369th Regiment and the other Black American units with open arms. The Black soldiers were immediately accepted. They were welcome in French homes and places of business. The French women also welcomed them, but when that happened, Jim Crow appeared in France. It appeared in an official document dated August 7, 1918, and issued by General John "Black Jack" Pershing, the Commander of the American Expeditionary Force. This document, entitled *Secret Information Concerning Black American Troops*, was distributed to the French forces. The document essentially stated the White Americans' disdain for their Black counterparts and asked the French to discourage relationships between Black American soldiers and the French population, in particular relationships with French women.[40] Jim Crow was now officially the policy of the American Expeditionary Force.

Despite the exemplary combat performance of Black units, African American soldiers in Europe were subjected to continuous racial slurs and harassment throughout the war. Blacks were referred to as *coons* and *niggers*. Whenever possible, repeating the experiences of the Civil War, they were assigned duties as labor battalions. Many of the White officers assigned to Black units had been found unfit for assignment to White units. Every effort was made to denigrate their performance. The failure of the 368th Regiment in a September 1918 battle in the Meuse-Argonne area was used as a prime example of Blacks' inability to fight and of Black inferiority. Only later, after a full investigation, was it revealed that the unit had been sent into battle without artillery support, maps, wire cutters, grenade launchers and other materials needed for an attack against fortified trenches.[41]

At the eleventh hour on the eleventh day of the eleventh month of the year 1918, the guns fell silent in Europe. The war to end all wars came to an end. The American Expeditionary Force returned home to a triumphant welcome by the City of New York. As the units of victorious soldiers paraded down Fifth Avenue, Jim Crow was evident by the lack of Black faces. Only later did the Black units return to hold their own parade. This time the parade route was in reverse. The 369th Infantry Regiment marched proudly up Fifth Avenue to Harlem.

Black America had heeded the call of W. E. B. Du Bois to close ranks.

It had sacrificed its sons to make the world safe for democracy while continuing to be the targets of insults and discrimination at home and abroad. With the war over Du Bois once again picked up his pen and expressed the feelings of Black Americans in an editorial, *Returning Soldiers*. He closed the editorial with these words: "Make way for Democracy! We saved it in France, and by the Great Jehovah, we will save it in the United States of America, or know the reason why." Du Bois' expectations of White America opening ranks and embracing Blacks for their sacrifices in World War I were not realized. Jim Crow continued to be the law of the land, and Whites resisted the new spirit of militancy among Black Americans. Frustrations and racial tensions mounted and exploded in a series of riots across the country.

❦

The year 1919 proved to be one of the bloodiest in the history of peacetime America. That summer, known as *The Red Summer*, there were 26 race riots. In many places, including the cities of Knoxville, Omaha, and Washington, D.C., the riots resembled battlefields.[42] In Chicago approximately 1,000 homes were burned, 15 Whites and 23 Blacks lost their lives and 600 were wounded. In addition to the riots there were 83 recorded lynchings in 1919. Those lynched included veterans wearing their uniforms; some were burned alive.[43]

The year 1919 also saw an increase in the membership and activities of the Ku Klux Klan. There were more than 200 public meetings of the Klan. Surprisingly, the meetings were held not only in the South, but also in New England, Florida, and Indiana. By the early 1920s, the Klan claimed a membership of approximately 4.5 million. The future for Black Americans appeared bleak. But then as the country entered the decade of the twenties by banning the sale of beer, wine, and distilled liquors, the *Jazz Age* began.

The Jazz Age with its flappers, speakeasies, and bootleg gin was a time for revelry and Harlem was the entertainment capital. Whites

The Ku Klux Klan has deep roots in the United States. This photograph, taken in 1926, shows Klansmen marching down Pennsylvania Avenue in the nation's capital. *Image courtesy of Documentary Photo Aids.*

would regularly come to Harlem to listen and dance to the music of Dizzy Gillespie, Charlie Parker and Duke Ellington. A famous song of the times, *Take the A Train,* captured the excitement and anticipation of White New Yorkers riding the subway as they headed for an evening of entertainment in Harlem. It was in Harlem that the sounds of modern jazz developed. The Harlem Renaissance soon followed.

Harlem of the 1920s was home for Black writers, artists, and musicians. It was in Harlem that W. E. B. Du Bois penned a collection of essays entitled *Darkwater.* Claude McKay published a book of poems, *Harlem Shadows.* Langston Hughes published his first book of poetry, *The Weary Blues.* Hall Johnson assembled a group of young singers to form what would become the famous Hall Johnson Choir. Aaron Douglass, later to become the head of the department of Fine Arts at Fisk University, painted murals for the Harlem YMCA and the New York Public Library. Harlem became the center of Black cultural activ-

97

ity and remains so today. In 1926, the Carnegie foundation purchased an extensive collection of Negro books from the Negro book collector Arthur Schomburg. This collection of books, in many languages, is located in the Harlem branch of the New York Public Library and serves as an important research center.

The Black Renaissance extended beyond Harlem. In 1921, Georgia Rosa Simpson at the University of Chicago, Sadie T. Moselland at the University of Tennessee, and Eva B. Dykes at Radcliffe College became the first Black women in the United States to receive doctorate degrees. In 1922, Roland Hayes, a classical singer, performed at Buckingham Palace for England's King George V. In 1923, Charles S. Johnson founded the magazine *OPPORTUNITY*, thus giving young Black writers an outlet for publishing their works. In 1926, Dr. Charles R. Drew, a graduate of Amherst College, became the chief surgeon at Freedman's Hospital in Washington, D.C., and became a leading authority on blood plasma. Throughout the decade Louis Armstrong and Lionel Hampton toured America with their bands.

In the short span of a half century, Black Americans, unshackled from the chains of slavery, had demonstrated their abilities in education, literature, politics, art, music, economics, and every other human endeavor. In the 1920s, Black versatility was personified in the personage of Paul Bustill Robeson. Robeson was born in 1898 in Princeton, New Jersey. In 1919, he graduated from Rutgers University. While at Rutgers, he was an honor student, an orator, and an athlete who earned twelve letters. In 1917, he was named an All-American football player. After graduation he went on to earn a law degree at Columbia University. Rather than pursue a career in law, he became a distinguished actor and singer. He was truly a Renaissance Man, an example of what Black Americans could accomplish if given the opportunity.

Robeson lived until 1976. Throughout his life he was politically active. In the 1930s he went to Europe to protest against the Nazis and to entertain loyalist troops in the Spanish Civil War. During the 1940s, Robeson starred on Broadway in *Othello*. After World War II, Robeson was caught in the anti-Communist hysteria of the McCarthy years. His passport was revoked, and he was denied the opportunity to perform in concert halls across America. In 1958 his passport was reissued and he departed for Europe just as his critically acclaimed book, *Here I Stand*, was being published. He remained in Europe performing on stage and in concert until 1963 when he returned to America and retired.[44]

The Jazz Age and the Harlem Renaissance produced important musicians, writers, and artists whose stars continue to shine brightly as the twenty-first century begins. However, the dominant charismatic public figure of the 1920s was a Jamaican immigrant who is little remembered outside the Black community. His name was Marcus Garvey.

❈

Marcus Garvey was born in Jamaica in 1887, the son of a carpenter. After an apprenticeship as a printer, Garvey went to England where he worked for an African Egyptian publisher. At night he studied at the University of London. In London he became increasingly aware of the problems and oppressions caused by colonialism. When he returned to Jamaica in 1914, he established the Universal Negro Improvement Association. The goals of this organization were to take Africa from the Imperialists and to make Africa the "defender of Negroes the world over." To further his efforts Garvey wanted to establish a school in Jamaica patterned after Tuskegee University. He corresponded with Booker T. Washington and eventually came to the United States to meet with him. When he arrived in America, Garvey learned that Washington had died and that the new president of Tuskegee, Robert Moton, disapproved of Garvey's concept of African nationalism.

Garvey settled in Harlem and preached his message of Africa for the Africans. Whites who were anxious to get rid of the Negro population in the United States immediately supported him. However, Garvey rejected any assistance from Whites. Rather, he denounced White philanthropy, criticized the integration policies of the NAACP, and directed his appeal to ordinary Black people. His message to the people was one of self-improvement and self-reliance. In speeches across the country he could be heard to say "Up, you mighty race. You can accomplish what you will." As a charismatic speaker Garvey was the predecessor of Martin Luther King, but his message of self-reliance was to be passed on by Malcolm X. Garvey was criticized by W. E. B. Du Bois and other intellectuals. He was characterized as a fake and a demagogue. Nevertheless, ordinary Blacks willingly supported his movement to the tune of $10,000,000.

In 1921, Garvey was at the height of his popularity. His Universal Negro Improvement Association sponsored a convention in New York City that was attended by Blacks from the United States, the West Indies, and Africa. The convention culminated in a mass rally of approximately 50,000 people at Madison Square Garden. Garvey announced the establishment of an African Republic with him as President. Its flag of Black, Red, and Green was symbolic of the Black race, the blood of the Black race, and the hopes of the Black race.

As an adjunct of his African Republic, Garvey created a chain of grocery stores, laundries, factories, and restaurants. His crowning achievement was the establishment of the Black Star Line, a shipping venture that would transport Black Americans back to Africa. Unfortunately, Garvey was a better speaker and dreamer than a businessman and the Black Star Line eventually failed.

In 1923, Garvey was arrested on charges of mail fraud. Convicted, he was sentenced to five years in prison. Branded as a danger to society, he was deported to Jamaica in 1927. He died in London in 1940.[45] Although many are quick to point to his failures, Garvey's legacy was his gift to the ordinary Black American of a sense of identity and self-worth. It was by no means a small gift.

❮

The Jazz Age crashed, along with the economy, on Tuesday, October 29, 1929, as the stock market plummeted. Black Tuesday marked the beginning of the Great Depression. Fortunes were lost overnight, jobs evaporated, bread lines and soup kitchens sprouted across the landscape. A new class of homeless people sought shelter in shanty towns. These communities of cardboard and wooden shacks were derisively known as *Hoovervilles.* They were named after the President the people blamed for the Depression. America entered a decade of economic despair and skyrocketing unemployment.

Last hired, first fired. The Depression of 1929 was particularly hard on Black Americans. *Image courtesy of Documentary Photo Aids.*

Unemployment is a cyclical event familiar to most Americans. What isn't generally appreciated is that in the 1930s, there was no safety net for the unemployed. There was no Social Security system or similar government program at the state level to assist those out of work. That's what separates the Great Depression from difficult times in the decades to follow. If people lost their jobs in 1929, they were without any means of supporting themselves or their family. As a result many resorted to begging.

If Black Tuesday was the beginning of difficult times for the rest of America, it marked the beginning of desperate times for Black America. The experience of Black Americans can be summed up in the quote "Last hired first fired." By 1937, approximately 26% of Black males were unemployed. Unemployment among Black women was even higher. Unlike Whites, many of whom worked on farms or could turn to relatives who had farms, Blacks had been increasingly living in cities and had no alternative refuge. However, they did have the Black community and the Black church to sustain them through this period. A shining example of a Black leader taking care of his own is the case of George Baker, better known as Father Divine. Father Divine established a series of religious cooperatives in the Eastern United States that provided food, shelter, and support for those in need. His teaching focused on decency, hygiene, and self-reliance. He encouraged literacy and honesty. His followers gave of their labor and their incomes according to their ability and received according to their needs. Father Divine's door was open to all regardless of color.[46]

❈

The Great Depression provided another opportunity for racism to flourish since it feeds on desperation. One incident stands out as an example of racism at its worst. History records the case simply as *The Scottsboro Boys*. On March 25, 1931, nine Black men were pulled from a freight train in Paint Rock, Alabama, ostensibly for having been involved in a fight with some White boys who were also riding the train. Hitching a ride on a freight train was not uncommon during the Depression. It became known in the lore of the times as riding the rails. The Blacks were arrested and taken to the county jail in Scotsboro.

When the sheriff's men searched the train, they also discovered two White women illegally aboard. This was unusual. Reputable women did not ride the rails. Assuming that these women were no accounts, the sheriff was about to charge them with vagrancy when the women claimed that they had been attacked and raped by the Black men. In that instant, these women of dubious reputation were transformed. They represented the sanctity of the White Southern belle, and nine Black brutes had violated them. Their honor had to be protected at all costs and it was. The words innocent until proven guilty, fair trial, and justice lost their meaning as all-White juries found the nine Black men guilty at three separate trials. And on each occasion the sentence was death.

The evidence in the case clearly proved the innocence of these men. One defendant was so stricken with syphilis that it was physically impossible for him to have engaged in intercourse. The physical examinations of the two women showed no evidence of a struggle or any recent sexual activity. At one of the trials, one of the accusers, Ruby Bates, recanted her story and said the rape had never occurred. Nevertheless, the verdicts came in Guilty—Guilty—and Guilty.

None of the Scottsboro Boys were ever put to death; however, they remained in jail for years as their cases were tried, appealed, tried, appealed, and tried again. They eventually regained their freedom, but it wasn't until November 29, 1976, some 45 years later, that the case finally came to an end. On that date the Alabama Board of Pardons and Parole granted Clarence Norris a complete pardon.

The fact that the Scottsboro Boys were Black and accused of raping two White women was in itself sufficient for an Alabama jury to find them guilty. However, the fact that they were being defended by a Jewish lawyer from New York and supported by the NAACP aggravated their plight. Jews were viewed almost as badly in Alabama as Negroes. When it became apparent that the United States Communist Party was also assisting, the fate of the Scottsboro Boys was sealed.

There was one other victim of the Scottsboro Boys case—a White judge by the name of James Edward Horton, Jr. Judge Horton was a respected member of his community, Decatur, Alabama. He had had a successful career and looked forward to a promising future. Then he was assigned as the presiding judge in the second trial of Hayward Patterson, one of the Scottsboro Boys. At the conclusion of the trial, the jury delivered the inevitable guilty verdict. The defense called for a mistrial and asked that Patterson be given a new trial. After considering the defense's motion and reviewing the evidence, Judge Horton granted the defense motion and set aside the verdict. With that decision Horton, an honest and principled man, lost his standing in his community. He was not re-elected to another term as judge and quietly passed into the annals of history.

There were, however, two positive results of the Scottsboro case. In the case of *Powell v. Alabama* the United States Supreme Court reaffirmed an accused's right to due process and a fair trial. In the case of *Norris v. Alabama* the Court ruled that it was unconstitutional to prevent Blacks from serving on a jury thus striking down the practice of trying Blacks before an all-White jury.[47]

❴

The hardships of the Great Depression molded the values of a generation of Americans. That generation practiced such ideals as helping a neighbor, saving for a rainy day, and sharing with the less fortunate. But the experience of the Depression also changed that generation's attitude toward government and its responsibility for the people.

America had been founded on the spirit of rugged individualism. The original colonists had faced hardship and survived. The pioneers of the Westward Movement had suffered privations, fought the Indians, and survived. Government played a small role in the lives of individual Americans. All that changed with the election of Franklin Delano Roosevelt in 1932. Roosevelt entered the White House in 1933 with 25% of the American labor force unemployed and a mandate from the American people to change the policies of government. He did so with a program he called *The New Deal*.

Roosevelt's New Deal created programs that put people to work building roads, dams, parks, etc. It created the Civilian Conservation Corps, a program to get young men off the streets, to put money in their pockets, and to burn up excess energy that might otherwise be ill spent. It created a Social Security system, which protected people out of work and provided the necessities of life for their families. For the first time, government was accepting responsibility to help those who could not help themselves.

Although Roosevelt's New Deal was not developed specifically for Black Americans, nevertheless they benefited from its programs. The National Youth Administration (NYA) is a good example. The NYA offered work to young people between the ages of 16 and 25. Its

Division of Negro Affairs was headed by Mary McLeod Bethune. Bethune, the daughter of ex-slaves, had previously founded and served as president of Bethune-Cookman College in Florida. When President Roosevelt appointed her to the NYA, Bethune became the first Black woman to head a federal office. Roosevelt's trust in her was well placed. Under her direction, the Division of Negro Affairs, through its student-work program, helped more than 60,000 young Black men and women learn a skilled trade.

As president, Franklin Roosevelt earned the respect of Black America. He appointed Blacks to significant positions within the New Deal. He listened to the advice of the Black leaders who soon earned the nickname of the *Black Cabinet*. His wife Eleanor was a civil rights activist in her own right.

Franklin Roosevelt also earned the votes of Black America. After the Civil War, Black voters had naturally favored the Republican Party, the party of Abraham Lincoln. In the 1930s the voting pattern of Black Americans shifted to the party of Franklin Roosevelt. Since then the Black vote has remained loyal to the Democratic Party. It should be remembered, however, that the switch of Black votes from the Republicans to the Democrats was a pragmatic decision based on the programs offered by the New Deal. Although now considered a Democratic constituency, the Black vote cannot be taken for granted by either party.

☾

The Great Depression in the United States also had an impact on the economies of Europe. This was particularly true in Germany which was still recovering from its defeat in World War I. Two forces were having a devastating impact on that country. First, the economy was unstable, unemployment was high, and people were hungry. Second, the Treaty of Versailles imposed restrictions on the army and forced Germany to accept blame for the war. The result was resentment, shame, and unrest among the German people. Many longed for the glory days of years past. The situation was ripe for a man named Adolph Hitler and his philosophy of Aryan supremacy. His message fell on eager ears and soon he was a powerful force in Europe.

By 1936, Hitler was trumpeting the virtues of White supremacy and his master race. He eagerly looked forward to the Olympic Games that year to be held in Berlin. Here was Hitler's chance to showcase his racial theory. Little did he know that a Black American by the name of Jesse Owens would in the course of a few seconds destroy the myth of the master race. Owens won four gold medals at the 1936 Olympics. Adolph Hitler left the stadium early to avoid the embarrassment of presenting the medals to the Black American. This was not the first time a Black American had exposed Hitler's racist theory of White supremacy. In June 1936, Joe Louis knocked out the German Heavyweight Max Schmeling in Yankee Stadium in New York City.

Joe Louis Barrow was born in Alabama on May 13, 1914, the son of sharecropping parents. He fought his first professional fight on July 4, 1934, in Chicago at the age of 20. Before Louis entered the ring Jack Blackburn, his manager, reminded him that he was a Black fighter in a White man's game. The best way to ensure that he won was to knock out his opponent. Louis went out and knocked out his White opponent, Jack Kracken, in the first round. The knockout was the first of many to come and soon became his trademark.

Professional boxing had for years been the exclusive domain of White fighters. Only one Black had dominated the sport, Jack Johnson. In the racial climate of his time, Johnson was a polarizing figure. Blacks were elated by his success. Whites resented each time he defeated one of their own. In 1913, Johnson moved to France to avoid a prison sentence. In 1915, he traveled to Cuba to fight Jess Willard. Whites were delighted when Willard won in 26 rounds. In 1920, Johnson returned to the United States and served out his prison sentence. On release from prison, he went into show business. Johnson died in a car accident in 1946. Years after his death he was elected to the International Boxing Hall of Fame.

From the outset Joe Louis was advised not to be a Jack Johnson. He wasn't. Louis had an illustrious boxing career which included holding the heavyweight championship for 12 years. More importantly, he became a symbol to Black and White youth alike. To a young Malcolm X, Louis was an example that the Black man could beat the White man. To Martin Luther King, Louis represented power for those who believed they were powerless. To the White youth of the 1930s, 1940s, and early 1950s, Joe Louis personified all that a champion should be. To most, the Brown Bomber was colorless. He was simply admired. After beating Louis in 1951, a sad Rocky Marciano said: "He was my idol."[48]

The tragedy of the Joe Louis story is that he was a good man who was used by many, including his country, and then was abandoned. Louis made substantial money in the ring, but he was a poor money manager. During World War II he joined the army where he performed countless exhibitions around the world in support of America's fighting men. After the war he was pursued by the Internal Revenue Service for failure to pay his taxes. By that time his skills had eroded and he should have retired, but his tax debt kept him chasing after paydays and ultimately forced him into professional wrestling. The spectacle of the once proud fighter performing as a wrestler was tragic. Ultimately he ended his days as a greeter at a Las Vegas casino. Nonetheless, people of all races were eager for the chance to shake his hand. Joe Louis never was a Jack Johnson. He was better—as a fighter, as a man. He was the first Black athlete to be embraced by the whole nation, and we are a better nation because he was one of us.

❲

December 7, 1941, will forever be remembered, in the words of Franklin Roosevelt, as a *Day of Infamy*. On that day the Japanese Empire conducted a surprise attack on the American fleet at Pearl Harbor. America was thrust into World War II.

For Black America World War II appeared to be a repeat of its predecessor, the one the United States fought to make the world safe for democracy in Europe while Mary Turner and 102 other Black Americans were lynched at home. As in World War I, many Black Americans immediately volunteered for service. Others were inducted through the selective service system. The military, however, remained segregated and racism ran rampant through the ranks. Nevertheless, despite overwhelming difficulties, the Black American again proved his exceptional ability in combat. Whites, however, generally had to find themselves in extreme circumstances before they were willing to acknowledge the bravery of Blacks. Two prime examples are the Tuskegee Airmen and the Montford Point Marines.

When the Tuskegee Airmen, the 99th Fighter Squadron, arrived in North Africa they were received with all the enthusiasm of their World War I predecessors, *Les Enfants Perdus.* Their introduction to combat came on July 2, 1943, when the Black pilots had their first encounter with their German opponents. On that day Lt. Charles B. Hall became the first Black pilot to shoot down a German plane. Sadly, July 2nd also is remembered as the day Lt. Sherman White and Lt. James McMullin became the first Black pilots to lose their lives in aerial combat.

The 332nd Fighter Group composed of the 100th, 301st, and 302nd Squadrons under the command of Benjamin O. Davis, Jr. was assigned to the Italian Theater of Operations. Later, the 99th Fighter Squadron joined the Group. Col. Davis had the tails of the Group's planes painted red. From their arrival in Europe in May 1944, until their deactivation in October 1945, the pilots known as the Tuskegee Airmen wrote a distinctive chapter in military history. The Germans feared the red tailed fighters and called then *Schwartze Vogelmenschen,* Black Birdmen. American bomber crews demanded that the Red Tails escort them because they knew their chance of survival was far greater with the Black pilots providing cover. In March 1945, the 332nd Group was awarded the Distinguished Unit Citation for escorting a flotilla of B-17s in an attack on Berlin. Although the American planes were subjected to fierce attacks by German fighters, including newly developed jet planes, the Black pilots repulsed the Germans with no American losses.[49]

While the Tuskegee Airmen overcame racism in the skies of North Africa and Europe, Black Marines attacked racism at home and the Japanese in the Pacific. Prior to World War II the Marine Corps refused to accept Negroes. In April 1941, as the United States prepared for the coming war, General Thomas Holcomb, the Commandant of the Marine Corps, expressed his opposition to recruiting Negroes. He said: "If it were a question of having a Marine Corps of 5,000 Whites or 250,000 Negroes, I would rather have the Whites."[50] The outbreak of war forced Holcomb to accept Blacks who were drafted into service. He reluctantly assigned them to segregated units and established a segregated Recruit Training Battalion. Black Marines would be trained at Montford Point, a remote portion of Camp Lejeune, North Carolina.

Black Marines assigned to Montford Point were commanded by White Officers. Fortunately their overall commander, Colonel Samuel A. Woods, Jr., was a fair man who earned the respect of his troops and mitigated the problems of segregation as best he could. Non-commissioned officers were ultimately to be Black Marines, but the shortage of trained Black NCOs made it necessary to initially assign Whites to the fill these tasks. Anticipating a problem, General Holcomb issued a letter of instruction in March 1943, which explained that it was "essential that in no case there be Colored non-commissioned officers senior to White men in the same unit, and desirable that few, if any, be of the same rank." Although General Holcomb retired as Commandant on January 1, 1944, this letter of instruction continued effectively to restrict the promotional opportunities of all Black Marines.

On June 15, 1944, the 4th Marine Division landed on the island of Saipan. Black Marines of the segregated 18th Marine Depot Company, a support unit, fought as infantrymen and repulsed a Japanese attack designed to drive the Marines back into the sea. Private Kenneth J. Tibbs of the 29th Marine Depot Company was killed in action that day; the first Black Marine to give his life for his country in World War II.[51] At the conclusion of the Saipan campaign the Black units assigned to the 4th Marine Division were awarded the Presidential Unit Citation.

The accomplishments of the Black Marines on Saipan were recognized by the new Commandant of the Marine Corps, Lieutenant General Alexander Vandergrift. General Vandergrift, who won the Medal of Honor at Guadalcanal, declared : "The Negro Marines are no longer on trial. They are Marines, period."[52] Nevertheless, Black Marines continued to be assigned to segregated units.

Black Marines also participated in the battles of Tinian and Peleliu, the recapture of Guam, and the invasion of Iwo Jima. They distinguished themselves in each of these conflicts. On Okinawa, the final battle of the war, Privates James M. Whitlock and James Davis were awarded the Bronze star for heroic achievement.[53] By the end of the war the Montford Point Marines had permanently shattered the exclusionary policies of the Marine Corps.

Other Black units were not as fortunate as the Tuskegee Airmen and the Montford Point Marines. The case of the 10th Cavalry is more typical of the Black experience in World War II. The 10th Cavalry had a long and proud history of service. First organized in 1866, the Regiment had seen service in the Indian Wars and had become known as the Buffalo Soldiers. Later they had fought with Teddy Roosevelt in the Spanish-American War. After World War I the Regiment had been assigned garrison and border patrol duties in the United States. All the while, they were commanded by White officers as military policy prohibited Black soldiers from rising above the rank of Sergeant. Many White officers considered assignment to a Black unit as the death knell on their careers. Leadership, therefore, was always a problem. During World War II the 10th Regiment was kept within the confines of the United States until 1944, when it was sent to North Africa. There the Regiment was disbanded. The troops were reassigned as engineers and truck drivers.

As World War II was drawing to a close, Adolph Hitler made one last desperate gamble to snatch victory from defeat. In December 1944, he massed his forces in Belgium and launched a massive surprise attack through the Ardennes Forest. The objective of the attack was to split the Allied forces, capture Paris, and hopefully bring the war to a conclusion on terms more favorable to the Germans. He almost succeeded in what came to be known as The Battle of the Bulge.

The German attack breached a weak point in the American lines and for a while the situation was desperate. The day after Christmas 1944, General Eisenhower, the Allied Supreme Commander, appealed to Black troops to volunteer as infantry replacements. He promised that they would be assigned, without regard to race, to units needing fighting replacements. At this point the American Army, for a moment, became integrated as Black troops fought and died alongside Whites in the successful effort to halt the German advance.[54] Ironically, after the war when Congress was considering the question of integrating the Armed Forces, General Eisenhower spoke out forcefully against integration. Sometimes memories are short.

❈

On the home front racism prevailed even though the country was mobilized for a wartime economy. Discrimination in defense contracts and jobs was commonplace. There were tensions in the factories as Southern Whites moved north seeking the well paying defense jobs. Fights were not uncommon. In June 1944, thirty-four people were killed in a riot in Detroit.

Racism appeared in other forms as well. One of the most popular songs of the times was bandleader Glenn Miller's "Chattanooga Choo Choo." This catchy song, sung by Tex Benekhe, opened with these lines: "Pardon me, boy, is that the Chattanooga Choo Choo? Track 29. Boy, you can give me a shine." For White America the line "Boy, you can give me a shine" was a catchy phrase. For Black America it was symbolic of a stereotypical attitude among Whites that Blacks were inferior. No matter what his age, the Black man would always be a *boy*. No matter what skills he possessed, he would always be confined to menial work. As White Americans sang and danced to the "Chattanooga Choo Choo," Black Americans chafed.

Nevertheless, despite continued segregation, racism, and discrimination, World War II marked a turning point for Black America. At the onset of World War I, W. E. B. Du Bois had appealed to Black America to close ranks and support the American effort in that war. He believed when the war ended Black Americans would be repaid for their sacrifices with the dismantling of Jim Crow. It did not happen. The new leaders of Black America, men like Asa Phillip Randolph, Adam Clayton Powell, and Thurgood Marshall, resolved that Black Americans would not shed their blood in World War II for nothing. This time they would demand their rights. Randolph was the first to act.

(

Asa Phillip Randolph was born in 1889 the son of a Florida minister. He had been active in the labor movement and was head of the Brotherhood of Pullman Car Porters. As the United States began to prepare for war in the late 1930s and 1940s, Randolph objected to the government awarding lucrative defense contracts to companies that refused to hire Blacks. Early in 1941, he proposed that 50,000-100,000 Black Americans march on Washington, D.C. to protest the government's actions. A protest march of this proportion was unheard of in those days. Naturally, President Roosevelt opposed the march, as did most of the White liberal community. The president summoned Randolph to the White House to discuss the matter. This was the equivalent of saying that Roosevelt intended to prevent the march. To the President's surprise, Randolph refused to call off the march unless Roosevelt promised immediate corrective action. On June 25, 1941, President Roosevelt issued Executive Order 8802 banning discrimination in industries holding government contracts and creating a Committee on Fair Employment Practices. This was the first Presidential Executive Order on race relations since the Emancipation Proclamation.[55] Randolph had succeeded and the quest for civil rights took a baby step.

Randolph was admired by the Black community and was considered a strong, fair-minded man who was good to his word. In 1944, people wanted to send him to Washington, D.C., to represent them in Congress. After considering his obligations to the Brotherhood of Pullman Porters and his personal disinclination for party politics, Randolph declined. Instead he gave his support to a young, charismatic, Harlem minister named Adam Clayton Powell.

Adam Clayton Powell, like his father before him, was the pastor of Harlem's Abyssinian Baptist Church. In addition to his pastoral duties, Powell was active in local politics, having won a seat on the New York City Council. He was a dynamic man, full of life and ideas with a genuine interest in improving the life of his people. His popularity is best reflected in the fact that in the congressional primary of 1944, Powell won both the Democratic and the Republican nominations, making the election in November a mere formality. In the Republican primary Powell, a Democrat, beat his Republican opponent by more than 350 votes. Thus began a congressional career that would span 26 years, a career that was, to say the least, mercurial.

Unfortunately, Powell is best remembered for incidents that occurred late in his career: frolicking with beautiful young women on the island of Bimini and an effort by members of the House of Representatives to deny him his seat. For years, however, Powell led the fight for civil rights. He was the outspoken spokesman for Black America. His message demanding equality, dignity, and economic opportunity was delivered during a time when the country was far less tolerant than it was during the civil rights years of the 1960s. In many ways Adam Clayton Powell paved the way for Martin Luther King, Jr.

❆

While Adam Clayton Powell pursued the cause of justice in the political arena, another man sought justice in the courts. His name was Thurgood Marshall. Thurgood Marshall was born in Baltimore, Maryland, in 1908. He graduated from Lincoln University and Howard Law School. He became the driving force in the efforts of the NAACP to obtain civil rights for Black Americans. On June 13, 1967, a Texan with a Southern drawl, President Lyndon Johnson, appointed Thurgood Marshall to the U.S. Supreme Court. The Senate confirmed his appointment on August 30, and Marshall became the first African American to sit on the Court. In the early 1900s, though, there was little indication that this strapping young man with a wild streak was about to embark on such a distinguished legal career.

Marshall grew up in a fairly comfortable situation. His mother was a teacher. His father held a variety of jobs ranging from a Pullman Car porter to a steward at a private White golf club. In his spare time Marshall's father would hang around the local courthouse listening to the various cases. He would return home in the evening and initiate a lively discussion on the merits of cases he particularly enjoyed. Thus from an early age Marshall was exposed to the challenge of the law. He also received an unintended exposure to and understanding of the U.S. Constitution that would serve him well in later life. While in high school Marshall was caught, along with some other students, in a prank for which he received an unusual punishment. The Principal isolated Marshall from the others in the school's furnace room. While in isolation, Marshall was required to memorize the Constitution. He never forgot the punishment or the detailed knowledge it provided him of a document he would rely on throughout his lifetime.

After graduating from law school, Marshall began a private practice. Fortunately for American history, the Great Depression doomed that adventure and led Marshall to accept a job with the Baltimore branch of the NAACP. At 26 years of age Marshall embarked on his crusade for civil rights, and his first target was the University of Maryland.

Marshall had been prevented from attending the University of Maryland Law School solely because he was Black. He was determined that no other student would suffer a similar fate. To do so he needed a challenge to the University's admission policies. Donald Murray, a graduate of Amherst College, became Marshall's test case. Murray applied for admission and was promptly turned down. Marshall and his former college professor, the esteemed Charles Houston, took the case to court on June 18, 1935. They won. And they won again on January 15, 1936, in appellate court. For the first time the legal system had acknowledged that the concept of separate but equal was a sham.[56]

Marshall's anger at Jim Crow was fueled by the Black experiences of World War II. Discrimination continued in the workplace. Worse yet, in 1942, was the wanton killing of Black citizens in riots across the country: Los Angeles, California; Beaumont, Texas; Mobile, Alabama; Newark, New Jersey; Philadelphia, Pennsylvania, and other places. In June 1943, in Detroit, Michigan, a riot broke out that claimed the lives of twenty-two Blacks and three Whites. Seven hundred were injured. Police were unable to quell the violence. In the view of Roy Wilkins of the NAACP, the police were responsible for perpetuating the violence by focusing their efforts solely against the Black community. Finally, President Roosevelt was forced to send in federal troops to restore order. The country was at war with itself when it was supposedly unified against the common enemies of Germany and Japan.

When World War II ended, Marshall watched as Blacks once again returned to an ungrateful country. He remembered instances of German prisoners of war riding first class on trains while Black men in uniform were segregated in Jim Crow cars. He remembered the Black experience after World War I and the lynching of returning veterans. He vowed that history would not be repeated. He would dismantle Jim Crow.

Dismantling Jim Crow posed an immediate threat to Marshall's life. In 1946 in Columbia, South Carolina, 25 Blacks had been charged with assault and intent to commit murder as a result of a riot. William Pillow and Lloyd Kennedy were the last to be tried. Marshall successfully defended Pillow and got a limited five-year sentence for Kennedy. After the trial a group of local Whites intercepted Marshall's car and forced him to accompany them to a remote spot by a river. They intended to lynch him. Fortunately, a group of armed Blacks intervened. This is but one of many instances where Marshall was willing to risk his life for his fellow man. It is symbolic of the courage Marshall displayed throughout his life. In the years that followed, Marshall continued to chip away at the Jim Crow laws. In 1947, he received help from an unexpected source. Branch Rickey, the White owner of the Brooklyn Dodgers, integrated the great American pastime of baseball by starting Jackie Robinson at second base.

Jackie Robinson was a marvelous athlete and a fiery competitor. He lettered in four sports at the University of California. He was also no stranger to racism. During World War II, while serving as a lieutenant in the United States Army, Robinson had been court-martialed for refusing to obey Jim Crow laws. Branch Rickey warned Robinson of the difficulties he could expect. He instructed Robinson not to respond to the insults that would surely come from fans, players, and even his own teammates. For a competitor like Robinson this was a Herculean task.[57] Nevertheless, he let his talent speak for itself, and by the end of that 1947 season, he had successfully integrated professional baseball. Through his talent, courage, and gentlemanly character Jackie Robinson made the work of Thurgood Marshall that much easier. In later years Martin Luther King, Jr., would attribute much of his own success to the efforts of Jackie Robinson.

In 1950, the U.S. Supreme Court handed down favorable rulings in three of Marshall's most critical cases. In *Sweatt v. Painter* the Court ruled that equality in education involved more than physical facilities. In this case the State of Texas, to meet the requirements for a separate but equal law school, had changed the name of the Black state college to Prairie View University. It had failed, however, to appropriate any funds to support the change. The Court reasoned that an equal education meant having the same qualified teachers, the same availability of texts and research materials, etc. In other words, equal meant just what it said—equal.

The second case involved the University of Oklahoma Graduate School and a Black professor, G.W. Mc Laurin, who wanted to get a doctorate in education. In this case the Court ruled that once a student had been admitted to a university he could not be segregated. No

In May 1954, in the case of *Brown* v. *The Board of Education of Topeka,* the Supreme Court of the United States in a unanimous decision reversed the 1896 *Plessy* v. *Ferguson* doctrine of *separate but equal. Image courtesy of Documentary Photo Aids.*

longer would Black students suffer the humiliation of being required to listen to lectures in a separate room adjacent to the White-only classroom. Imagine trying to absorb the nuances of a professor's lecture when you're not even in the same room. Equally important, all facilities of the university were now open to students of color.

The third case struck at the very soul of Jim Crow. In the case of Elmer Henderson, the Court banned segregation in railroad dining cars. Finally, one of the basic props of segregation had been shattered. There would be, however, many more years of struggle, years of humiliation, years of lynching, and years of unflinching resolve before the taboos of inter-racial eating and inter-racial marriage would be overcome.

As Marshall successfully attacked segregation in higher education, there were new stirrings at the secondary level. The inequities of segregated schools were too blatant to escape the attention of Black parents and students. In 1951, Barbara Johns and her 15-year-old sister Joan staged a walkout at the all-Black Morton High School in Farmville, Virginia. The girls were protesting the terrible condition of their school, a tarpaper building that held out neither the winter cold nor the seasonal rains. In Summerton, South Carolina, Black parents petitioned in court to end educational inequality, and in Charleston. Harry Briggs sought to end segregation in his child's school district by asking Thurgood Marshall to take his case to court.

On a sunny September day in 1950, in Topeka, Kansas, Oliver Brown took his seven-year-old daughter Linda by the hand and went for a walk. Their destination was the all-White Sumner School. Arriving at the school, Oliver Brown attempted to enroll Linda. She was rejected. Brown's attempt to enroll Linda in the Sumner School wasn't an overt attempt to desegregate the school system. He was simply fed up with the fact that Linda had to walk through a dangerous railroad yard to catch an unreliable bus that would then take her to the all-Black Monroe school about a mile away. Earlier a registration notice had been placed in the doors, including the Browns', of all students living in the Sumner School District. Brown saw the registration notice as an invitation and as an opportunity for his child. When the school rejected Linda, Brown took his case to the NAACP. Little did he realize that he and Linda would become the central figures in the United States Supreme Court's most momentous decision of the twentieth century.

On Monday May 17, 1954, the United States Supreme Court, under the leadership of Chief Justice Earl Warren, rendered its decision in the case of *Brown v. the Board of Education of Topeka*. The Court concluded that "in the field of public education, the doctrine of separate but equal has no place." The previous decision rendered in *Plessy v. Ferguson* had been overturned. The doctrine of separate but equal had been repudiated. Oliver and Linda Brown, the NAACP, and every Black man and woman in the United States had prevailed. For that, they could thank Thurgood Marshall.

NOTES

25. Bennett, p. 261

26. Bennett, p. 352

27. John Hope Franklin.,ed., *Three Negro Classics; Up From Slavery, The Souls of Black Folk, the Autobiography of an Ex-Colored Man.*(New York: Avon, 1965) pp.56-57

28. Louis R. Harlan, *Booker T. Washington the Wizard of Tuskegee, 1901-1915* (New York: Oxford University press, 1983), p. 135

29. David Levering Lewis, *W. E. B. Du Bois: Biography of a Race* (New York: Henry Holt and Company, 1993, p. 165

30. Daniel Boorstin and Kelley Brooks, *A History Of The United States; Since 1861* (New Jersey: Prentice Hall, 1989), p. 179

31. Boorstin and Kelley, p. 172

32. Lewis, pp. 331-332

33. Low and Clift, pp. 491-496

34. Bennett, p. 342

35. Hughes, Meltzer, & Lincoln, pp. 272-276

36. Lewis, p. 423

37. Hughes, Meltzer, & Lincoln, p. 267

38. Lewis, pp. 532-535

39. Bennett, p. 348

40. Lewis, p. 572

41. Lewis, p. 571

42. Bennett, p. 353

43. Hughes, Meltzer, & Lincoln, p. 267

44. W. Augustus Low, and Virgil A. Clift, eds., *Encyclopedia of Black America* (New York: McGraw-Hill Inc., 1981), p. 732

45. Hughes, Meltzer, & Lincoln, pp. 270-271

46. Hughes, Meltzer, & Lincoln, p. 282

47. James Haskins, *The Scottsboro Boys* (New York: Henry Holt and Company, 1994), p. 105

48. "Joe Louis," *The Lincoln Library of Sports Champions,* 1974 Vol. 11, p. 61

49. C.V. Giles, "The Red-Tailed Fighters," *The Retired Officer Magazine, Volume XLVIII No. 9,* (September 1992), pp. 26-29

50. Marine Corps Historical Center, *THE RIGHT TO FIGHT: African Americans in World War II,* Washington, D.C., 1995, p. 1

51. Marine Corps Historical Center, p. 20

52. Marine Corps Historical Center, p. 21

53. Marine Corps Historical Center, p. 24

54. Merideth R. Vezina, "In Limbo at Lockett," *The Retired Officer Magazine, Volume L, No. 2* (February 1994), p. 32

55. Bennett, p. 356

56. Carl.T Rowan, *Dream Makers, Dream Breakers; The World of Justice Thurgood Marshall* (Boston: Little Brown and Company, 1993), pp. 50-52

57. "Jackie Robinson," *The Lincoln Library Of Sports Champions,* 1974 Vol.8, pp. 20-27

5

Martin Luther King, Jr.
through Affirmative Action

Historians conveniently call the 1950s the decade of the Silent Generation. Nothing could be further from the truth. Admittedly there was a Silent Generation. It was the middle and upper class college students whose focus was narrowed by isolation on campuses across the nation. To them the important issues of the day were how many students could be stuffed into a Volkswagen or when the next panty raid was scheduled.

For Black Americans, the decade of the fifties was far different. It was a time when many were forced from passive acceptance of the status quo to organized protest for their civil rights. It was a time when Blacks were portrayed on television only as domestic servants or comic characters. Rochester, the genial chauffeur on *The Jack Benny Show*, typified the portrayal of Blacks on television and in the movies. Segregation continued to be the norm in the North and South with respect to education, jobs, and housing.

The 1950s was also a time of fear for all Americans. Communism was the common enemy abroad and the House Un-American Activities Committee and Senator Joseph Mc Carthy were the enemies at home.

Ironically, the fight for Black civil rights was given impetus on June 25, 1950, when 60,000 North Korean soldiers crossed the 38th parallel and invaded South Korea. The United States sent troops to assist the South Koreans. For the first time, America sent an integrated army into combat.

After World War II, demobilization of the Armed Forces forced Congress to review the future roles and missions of the services. The result of this review was the National Security Act of 1947. This act defined the missions of the Army, Navy, and Marine Corps. It also created a new branch of service, the U.S. Air Force, and the Office of the Joint Chiefs of Staff. It did not, as many had hoped, integrate the Armed Forces. This failure was due in large part to the congressional testimony of former General of the Army Dwight D. Eisenhower. General Eisenhower, despite the performance of Black troops during the Battle of the Bulge, clung to the antiquated position that to integrate the services would be prejudicial to good order and discipline.

President Harry Truman had succeeded Franklin Roosevelt after Roosevelt died in the spring of 1945. Truman had authorized use of the atomic bombs to end World War II. He was viewed by the American public as a good and fair man, but not one of particularly high intelligence or political acumen. In the election of 1948, Truman was challenged by Governor Thomas Dewey of New York. Truman was given little chance of being returned to the White House because the Democratic Party was sharply divided over the issue of civil rights.

Although he was from Missouri, Truman supported civil rights and insisted that it be included in the Democratic Party's platform for the 1948 election. In addition, on July 26, 1948, he issued a Presidential Executive Order integrating the Armed Forces. In truth it must be said that he did so, in part, to appeal to Black voters for the coming election. It is equally true, however, that he did so out of conviction that integration of the services was the right thing to do.

Truman's integration order was not universally welcomed. Military commanders, many of whom were graduates of Southern military institutions, were slow to embrace integration. Some blatantly resisted it. Once again retired General Dwight Eisenhower testified before the Senate Armed Services Committee. He repeated his belief that small units, in particular, should not be integrated.

Although the official policy of the United States was an integrated Armed Force, the U. S. Army in Korea remained in many ways a segregated organization. Reports of racism, discrimination, and the flagrant abuse of Black soldiers' rights within the military justice system reached Thurgood Marshall, and he embarked on a fact-finding trip to Korea. When Marshall arrived at Army Headquarters in Tokyo, he was cordially greeted by the Commander in Chief, General Douglas MacArthur. Marshall was given a series of briefings that, while on the surface appeared to be factual, nonetheless left him wary. When he arrived on the front lines in Korea his worst suspicions were confirmed. Of particular concern to Marshall was the Army's proclivity for charging Black soldiers with "misbehavior before the enemy," which in layman's terms translates into cowardice. Between August and October 1950, thirty-two Black soldiers and two White soldiers were so charged. Marshall found it hard to believe that Blacks were that more cowardly. He concluded that Jim Crow was at work. [58]

Jim Crow was not limited to overseas units. Back in the United States the NAACP received complaints from Fort Bliss, Texas, that White soldiers were being sent to Europe while Blacks were sent to Korea. At a camp in Indiana, the Commanding Officer had assembled the troops and told them there would be no mixing of the races. In Alabama at Camp Rucker, Blacks continued to live in segregated barracks and were generally harassed by the White population whenever they went into town. Five Fort Benning soldiers were arrested after a fight with police in Columbus, Georgia. One of the soldiers was beaten by the police so badly that his friends thought he was dead.

The war in Korea once again confirmed the courage and fighting qualities of Black soldiers in battle. On June 2, 1951, at a place called Chipo-ri, Sergeant Cornelius H. Charlton, a member of Company C of the 24th Infantry Division, assumed command of his rifle platoon when the platoon leader was killed. At the time the platoon was attacking a heavily defended enemy hill. During the attack Charlton was severely wounded. He refused medical attention and continued to lead his men in the assault. At a critical point in the battle, Charlton spotted an enemy emplacement that was preventing his unit from capturing an important ridgeline and was inflicting heavy casualties on his unit. Charlton charged the emplacement. During this attack he was severely wounded by an enemy grenade. Nevertheless, he continued to attack and captured the position after killing several of the enemy and forcing the remainder to flee. Cornelius Charlton was awarded the Congressional Medal of Honor for his bravery. He also died of his wounds.[59]

The war in Korea was also a turning point in the history of Jim Crow. The undeniable fact was that the President of the United States had made equal treatment of all persons in the Armed Forces official policy. Thurgood Marshall and the NAACP fought to enforce that policy. The seed had been planted that nearly 40 years later would bloom with the appointment of Colin Powell as Chairman of the Joint Chiefs of Staff. He was the first African American entrusted with the responsibility for the defense of our nation.

C

The May 17, 1954 decision of the Supreme Court in the case of *Brown v. the Board of Education of Topeka* failed to establish a specific time for integrating public school systems. The absence of a deadline opened the door for creative plans designed to delay, if not deny, the admission of Black children into White schools. Virginia argued that implementation of any desegregation plan must be predicated on the ability of the community to change attitudes. In many Southern states White citizens' councils were formed to continue segregation by establishing private schools. On May 31, 1955, Chief Justice Warren delivered the Court's unanimous opinion with respect to implementation of the Brown decision. Once again the Court avoided setting a specific

An integrated classroom in Fort Myer, Virginia after the school was deseg-regated in 1954. *Image courtesy of Documentary Photo Aids.*

date for implementation. Instead, it instructed the lower courts to act with all deliberate speed in desegregation cases.

"All deliberate speed" is a phrase subject to wide interpretation. It sat-isfied practically no one. In some cases it meant immediate implemen-tation of desegregation. In others it meant years of foot dragging and obstruction. However, in retrospect, the phrase did result in two major accomplishments. First, it left implementation of the law squarely in the hands of the local Federal Judges. For the most part, these judges were reasonable, thoughtful individuals who would try to meet the spirit and intent of the Supreme Court's decision. Second, by allowing latitude in implementation, notwithstanding the abuses that were bound to occur, it prevented outright rebellion and organized violence.[60]

In the wake of the Brown decision, inflammatory rhetoric by the Ku Klux Klan and other extremists created an atmosphere of tension and hate throughout the South. Violence was bound to follow. On August

21, 1955, Clarence Jones and Emmett Till, teenagers from Chicago, boarded a train to visit their relatives in Money, Mississippi. The boys were looking forward to picking cotton. Jones had boasted to his mother that he could pick 200 pounds in one day. A few days after arriving in Money, Emmett Till was showing pictures of his Chicago classmates to his new friends. Emmett pointed out a pretty young White girl he claimed as his girl friend. After seeing the picture, one of the group dared Emmett to speak to the White lady who ran the local general store. Emmett entered the store and made a small purchase. On leaving he said to the White lady, "Bye, baby." That night two men came to the house where Emmett was staying and took him away. He was never again seen alive. Several days later his disfigured body, which had been tied to an iron wheel, was recovered from the Tallahatchie River. For speaking to a White woman, Emmett had been brutally beaten and shot through the head. The men accused of the murder, two Klansmen, were acquitted by an all-White jury.

❰

Two months after Emmett Till was murdered, Rosa Parks, a seamstress by profession, completed her work as a volunteer secretary for the NAACP and left her office to go home. It was December 1, 1955. She boarded a public bus at Court Square in Montgomery, Alabama, and took her seat. It had been a long, busy day.

In 1955, the public buses in Montgomery were segregated. Blacks were required to sit in a section in the rear of the bus specifically designated for coloreds. The law also required Blacks to give up their seats should the White section become full. When the bus stopped at the Empire Theater, a number of White people got on board completely filling the White section. One White man was standing without a seat. Seeing the White man standing, the bus driver, James Blake, commanded the people in the front row of the Black section to vacate their seats. Nobody moved. After a second, more threatening warning, one man and two women stood up. Rosa remained seated. Seeing that Rosa was still sitting, the driver asked her if she was going to move. Rosa replied she was not.

This was not the first confrontation between James Blake and Rosa Parks. Twelve years earlier he had put her off his bus for failing to board through the rear door. At that time Blacks were required to enter the bus at the front door, pay their fare, then get off the bus and re-enter through the back door to take their seat. In the 1943 incident Rosa had refused to get off and re-enter the bus. She waited for another bus, vowing never again to board a bus driven by Blake. Unfortunately, in 1955 Rosa was preoccupied with thoughts of her work at the NAACP and didn't notice that he was the bus driver. This time, though, Rosa's resolve was firm. Over the years she had had her fill of the degrading humiliation of segregation. Blake then said he would have Rosa arrested. She remained seated. He accepted her challenge; and soon two policemen arrived, took her to the police station, booked her, and placed her in a holding cell. She was later released on bail and finally arrived home at about 10:00 that night. It had indeed been a long day.

Rosa was not the first woman arrested in 1955 for refusing to give up her seat on a bus. Earlier a teenager named Claudette Colvin had been similarly arrested. News of Rosa's arrest spread through the Black community. A local women's political action group started handing out leaflets encouraging a boycott of the bus system on the day that Rosa would be tried. Resentment of the treatment they received at the hands of the bus system ran deep in the Black community. However, no one, Black or White, realized how deep.

Mr. Edgar D. Nixon was a leading activist in the Montgomery Black community. His résumé included leadership in the local branch of the Brotherhood of Sleeping Car Porters and the NAACP. For a long time he had been looking for the right person or incident to challenge the segregation laws in Montgomery. Claudette Colvin's arrest appeared to be an opening for a challenge. However, Claudette was unmarried and pregnant. She didn't appear to be the ideal candidate to face the public scrutiny that would inevitably accompany any challenge to the segregation laws. Rosa Parks was another matter. She was without blemish. She was a forty-two year old married woman, gainfully employed, without a police record whose only fault was that she was Black. In addition, she had been Nixon's friend and co-worker for many years. He asked if she would be willing to be the plaintiff in a test of the segregation laws. She accepted.

Nixon immediately set the wheels in motion that resulted in the now famous Montgomery Bus Boycott. His first call was to the Reverend Ralph Abernathy, minister of the First Baptist Church. Nixon then called 18 other ministers and arranged a meeting to discuss the situation and formulate plans for a boycott of the bus system. Then he contacted Joe Azbell, a White reporter for the *Montgomery Advertiser*, and asked for his help.

The meeting of the ministers concluded with the issuance of a leaflet that asked Blacks not to ride the buses on Monday, December 5th, the day of Rosa's trial. It also called for a mass meeting to be held at the Holt Baptist Church at 7:00PM Monday. The leaflet was designed for distribution throughout the community and to serve as the basis of sermons in every Black church on Sunday, December 4th. Azbell also used it in the lead story of the Sunday edition of the *Montgomery Advertiser*. This ensured that word of the protest would reach even those folks who didn't regularly attend church.

It is important to note here the role played by the Black church at the onset of this first organized protest for civil rights. Ministers provided the leadership. The church buildings provided the meeting halls. The congregations provided the support. It was a natural blending of the secular and spiritual communities that would prove to be so effective and important in the struggles that lay ahead.

On Monday, December 5th, Rosa Parks appeared in court as scheduled. She was found guilty of violating the segregation laws and was required to pay a $10.00 fine and $4.00 in court costs. That day, somewhat to the surprise of Edgar Nixon and the other leaders, the Black community united and refused to ride the buses. Black cab drivers transported people for the 10-cent bus fare instead of the 40-cent cab fare. People used car pools or simply walked to work. The buses were empty.

On that same day Ralph Abernathy, Edgar Nixon, a local attorney, Fred Gray, and some other ministers met and decided to form a new organization to be called the Montgomery Improvement Association. They felt this new organization would be free of any stigma attached to existing organizations, such as the NAACP. Also, and perhaps more importantly, a new local organization could more easily refute the standard White accusations of outside agitators causing trouble. The Reverend Martin Luther King, Jr., the young pastor of the Dexter Avenue Baptist Church, was selected as president of the new organization.

Martin Luther King, Jr. was fairly new to the Montgomery area, having assumed his pastoral duties in 1954, after completing his doctoral work at Boston University. However, Abernathy and the others considered King's recent arrival in Atlanta to be a strength; he had not been influenced by the local White community. He was only 26 years old when he assumed leadership of the Montgomery Improvement Association.

King was born in 1929, and grew up in the environs of Atlanta, Georgia, the son of a Baptist minister and a school teacher. He was a bright young man who skipped both the ninth and twelfth grades. He was admitted to Morehouse College at the age of fifteen and graduated in 1948, with a BA degree in sociology. A year earlier he had been ordained a minister in his father's church. After graduating from Morehouse, he attended Crozier Theological Seminary in Pennsylvania and then Boston University. While there, he met his future wife, Coretta Scott. At the time she was studying voice at the New England Conservatory of Music. They married and he assumed his duties at the Dexter Avenue Baptist Church. The church was located in downtown Montgomery directly across the street from the Alabama State House from which proudly flew the Confederate flag. During his first year at Dexter Avenue, King completed his thesis and received his doctorate from Boston University.

President Eisenhower poses in his White House office with four Black leaders on June 23, 1958, following their conference concerning school integration and other significant matters affecting Blacks. L to R: Dr. Martin Luther King, Jr., President of the Southern Christian Leadership Conference; E. Frederic Morrow, Administrative Officer, White House; President Eisenhower; A. Philip Randolph, Vice President, AFL-CIO; William P. Rogers; Rocco Siciliano, Special Assistant to the President; Roy Wilkins, Executive Secretary of the NAACP. *Image courtesy of Documentary Photo Aids.*

While a student at Morehouse, Crozier, and Boston University, Martin Luther King, Jr. was exposed to the ideas and philosophies of Thoreau, Reinhold Niebuhr, Ghandi and others. From the teachings of these scholars, King concluded that his ministry had to go beyond the spiritual and include a direct concern for the daily problems of his parishioners. It became clear to him that as a minister his theological responsibilities extended to the secular community. From this conviction he developed his concept of non-violent protest for which he would win the Nobel Peace Prize.[61]

At its first public meeting the Montgomery Improvement Association adopted a list of three demands to present to the bus company and to the White city officials:

- Courteous treatment on the buses;
- First come, first served seating, with Whites in front and Blacks in back;
- The hiring of Black bus drivers for bus routes in the Black community.

Following the meeting Dr. King and attorney Fred Gray met with three city officials and representatives of the Bus Company on December 8, 1955.[62] The demands were rejected, and the extended Montgomery bus boycott began.

The Montgomery bus boycott lasted over a year. During that time, Blacks adapted to their transportation needs with ingenuity. An intricate system of private transportation was developed complete with schedules, pick up stations, and transfer sites. Many people simply walked. Police and city officials responded with injunctions and harassment tactics. Some Whites responded with violence. In January 1956, the homes of Martin Luther King and Edgar D. Nixon were bombed. On the other hand, some White women assisted the boycott by transporting their maids to and from their homes. Segregation was one thing, but for these women a clean home was far more important.

On November 13, 1956, the U. S. Supreme Court upheld a lower court's ruling banning segregation on city buses. On December 20, 1956, federal injunctions were served on the City of Montgomery, the State of Alabama, and bus company officials prohibiting segregation on buses. The next day Dr. King boarded a bus and took a seat of his choice. So, too, did Rosa Parks. She was asked by reporters from *Look* magazine to board several buses that day for picture purposes. One of the buses she boarded was driven by none other than her former nemesis James Blake.

The success of the Montgomery boycott thrust Martin Luther King, Jr., into the civil rights movement and the national spotlight. Shortly thereafter King moved to Atlanta and established the Southern Christian Leadership Conference, a group dedicated to non-violent protest. In May 1957, King delivered his famous "Give Us the Ballot" speech at a prayer pilgrimage in Washington, D.C. He was now a national figure and had developed his plan of attack for civil rights.[63] It was based on four principles:

- Exercise the right to vote;
- Boycott businesses that practiced segregation;
- Use the Courts to protect civil rights;
- Participate in non-violent protest.

❮

King's emergence as a civil rights leader wasn't the only important event of the remarkable year of 1957. In July, Althea Gibson became the first Black American to win All England Tennis Championship at Wimbledon. She followed that achievement by becoming the first Black American to win the American National Tennis Championship by defeating Louise Brough 6-3,6-2 at Forest Hills that August. Then in September, nine Black students attempted to enter the segregated high school in Little Rock, Arkansas. What followed, according to Lerone Bennett, Jr., was the beginning of the *Second Reconstruction.* [64] Bennett's choice of the term Second Reconstruction is most appropriate. After the Civil War ended the federal government was forced to send troops into the South to protect the newly freed Black Americans. That period from 1867-1877 is known as the Reconstruction. Now in 1957 and for the next ten years the federal government would again be forced to deploy federal troops to protect its Black citizens.

Little Rock, Arkansas, population 107,333, was an unlikely setting for one of the early and dramatic confrontations of the civil rights movement. It was a moderate city in a moderate state. Early in 1957, the Little Rock School Board had approved a plan for nine black teenagers to integrate Central High School. The Governor of Arkansas was Orval Faubus, a moderate by Southern standards. However, it was an election year and Faubus knew that he would need the support of the segregationists if he were to be re-elected to a third term. On the night prior to the opening of school, Faubus decided that he would resist integration. That night he activated the National Guard. Its mission was to prevent the nine Black teenagers from enrolling at Little Rock's Central High School the following morning.

On September 5, 1957, eight of the nine Black teenagers arrived at the Central High School. They were accompanied by their parents and ministers. The National Guard, in full combat regalia, surrounded the school. What happened next hadn't occurred since General Lee surrendered at Appomattox Court House. The Black students were prevented from entering the school by armed troops in defiance of federal law.

The ninth student, Elizabeth Eckford, had failed to accompany the other students to school. Unfortunately, she arrived alone that morning. As she approached the school, she was followed by a hostile mob that threatened to kill her. It may well have succeeded, except for a brave middle-aged White woman who protected Elizabeth. The woman accompanied Elizabeth to a bus stop and put her on a bus and out of danger.

As the stand-off continued and as scenes of mob violence flashed onto television screens in living rooms across the country, President Eisenhower conferred with Governor Faubus in Washington. Eisenhower thought they had reached an agreement to integrate the schools. For his part Faubus returned to Arkansas and deactivated the National Guard. That left the future protection of the nine Black students the responsibility of the local police. It was soon apparent that the police were unable and in some cases unwilling to do the job. Finally, President Eisenhower ordered the 101st Airborne to Little Rock, and on September 25, 1957, the nine Black students accompanied by armed soldiers with bayonets drawn entered Central High School.

Entering the school was one thing. Going to school was quite another. The hostility within the student body was so extreme that each Black student was assigned an armed soldier as an escort. Nevertheless, there were some places the soldiers' could not provide protection. In a 1997 *Newsweek* interview Gloria Ray Karlmark said she never entered the girls bathroom that whole first year because it was too dangerous.

As the school year progressed, tensions were bound to erupt. One day in the lunchroom as Minnijean Brown was getting her food, a White boy continually harassed her. Without warning Minnijean dumped a bowl of chili over the boy's head, and in the stunned silence that followed the White students learned for the first time that Blacks would retaliate if pushed too far. The silence was finally broken by the applause of the Black cafeteria workers. Minnijean was expelled.[65]

During the course of the year, the Black students would gather each morning at the home of Daisy Bates, the local leader of the NAACP, and then go to school in a convoy of military jeeps, machine guns mounted on the lead and rear vehicles. As the year came to a close, two significant events took place. Craig Rains, a White student, began to have a change in attitude. He realized that the Black students had a right to the same opportunities that were available to him. He also began to resent those Whites who were continually disrupting the school and flaming the fires of hatred.[66] Then, on May 29,1958, Ernest Green received his diploma and became the first Black graduate of Central High School. He would go on to a successful business career. In 1958, Governor Orval Faubus closed the public school system in Arkansas. He was elected to a third term.

On September 25, 1997, Jefferson Thomas, Ernest Green, Minnijean Brown Trickey, Carlotta Walls La Nier, Terrence Roberts, Gloria Ray Karlmark, Thelma Mothershed-Wair, Elizabeth Rockford, and Melba Patillo Beals returned to Central High School. Forty years had passed. This time there was no vicious crowd. This time the President of the United States, Bill Clinton, greeted them. He, along with the Governor of Arkansas and the mayor of Little Rock, escorted the "Little Rock Nine" into the building. There wasn't a bayonet in sight.

The sight of the President of the United States escorting the nine middle-aged men and women into Central High School provided dra-

In 1957, nine Black students attempted to integrate Central High School in Little Rock, Arkansas. Governor Orval Faubus used the National Guard to prevent them from entering. On September 24th, President Eisenhower federalized the state militia and ordered 1,000 paratroopers from the 101st Airborne Division to Little Rock to supervise integration of the school. Despite the presence of the soldiers White crowds harassed the nine Black students. The above picture shows Jefferson Thomas waiting for transportation to his home. *Image courtesy of Documentary Photo Aids.*

matic coverage for the television and print media. It reinforced the achievements of the civil rights movement and offered an opportunity for America to rededicate itself its creed that "all men are created equal." However, it didn't tell the story of the terrible price these nine men and women paid to receive an education that was rightfully theirs. At the very moment when they should have been enjoying the fun and exuberance of being a teenager, they had been forced to carry the burden of a nation.

Melba Beals wrote a book about her experience, *Warriors Don't Cry*. She also spent twelve years in therapy. Elizabeth Eckford tried to write a book but couldn't. It was too painful. For years, Jefferson Thomas avoided crowds and would not attend football games, watch a parade, or tell his children of his role in the civil rights movement. His son learned about his father at school and was angry that his dad had not told him. Similarly, Gloria Karlmark told her children about the civil rights movement but omitted any mention of her role. Karlmark still recalls hearing FBI agents tell her parents that Gloria should be fingerprinted in case she needed to be identified later. The price was indeed high.

(

Five years earlier in August 1952, the gates of the prison in Charlestown, Massachusetts, opened and Malcolm Little walked out a free man. He had completed paying his price for previous careers as a pimp, thief, numbers runner, dope dealer, and other miscellaneous adventures in violation of the law. Soon the world would know him as Malcolm X. While serving a ten-year sentence for armed robbery, Malcolm Little educated himself by reading every book in the prison library. His thirst for knowledge was insatiable. He spent hours reading on subjects ranging from mathematical theories to the classics. One day his brother visited. He told Malcolm about a new religion that had changed his life and of its chief minister, Elijah Muhammed. Malcolm could readily see the change in his brother. Soon Malcolm was corresponding daily with Elijah Muhammed, eagerly asking questions about this new religion that championed the Black man. On release from prison, Malcolm went to hear him speak in Chicago. He had already accepted Muhammed's message that the White man was the devil. In Chicago, Malcolm became Elijah's disciple. Malcolm joined Temple Number One in Detroit. He renounced his last name, a name he felt was given to his family by slave owners, and replaced it with the Muslim X, which represented his true, yet unknown, family name.

Malcolm X's assignment at Temple Number One was to recruit converts to this religion that rejected drugs, prostitution, and alcohol—all the vices that Malcolm X had known so well. He approached his task with the same vigor and determination that he had used when reading in the prison library. His familiarity with the sins, habits and language of the streets became his greatest asset as a recruiter. In a short time he had tripled the membership of Temple Number One and caught the eye of Elijah Muhammed.

Malcolm X moved to New York and established a flourishing temple in Harlem. His life was devoted to spreading the Muslim message and by the early 1960s, he was the leading spokesman for the Nation of Islam. His message was simple. He preached that the White man was the enemy, that the Black man was superior, and that separation of the races, not integration, was best for the Black American.

When asked if he was preaching a philosophy of violence, Malcolm X responded that he wasn't. He went on to say, however, that if the White man continued to come into the Black community to rape Black women and commit other crimes, then he believed Blacks should respond with whatever means were necessary.[67] This response and Malcolm X's philosophy of separation was exactly opposite to the philosophy, of non-violence and integration being espoused by Martin Luther King, Jr. The White community was afraid of Malcolm X and naturally supported Dr. King.

By the mid-sixties Malcolm X was so popular that he was beginning to overshadow Elijah Muhammed. Within the Nation of Islam, this was unacceptable and Malcolm X was disciplined for insubordination. Malcolm X accepted his punishment and most likely would have continued his ministry had he not learned that Muhammed had committed adultery and fathered several children out of wedlock. Malcolm X was shattered by this revelation. When confronted by Malcolm X, Muhammed admitted his indiscretions. Malcolm X then returned to his mosque in New York and informed its members of the situation. Malcolm X's enemies now portrayed him as being disloyal. Eventually, Malcolm X learned of a plot to kill him. He knew only one man could approve of an attempt on his life. Malcolm X's days as Elijah Muhammed's disciple came to an end.

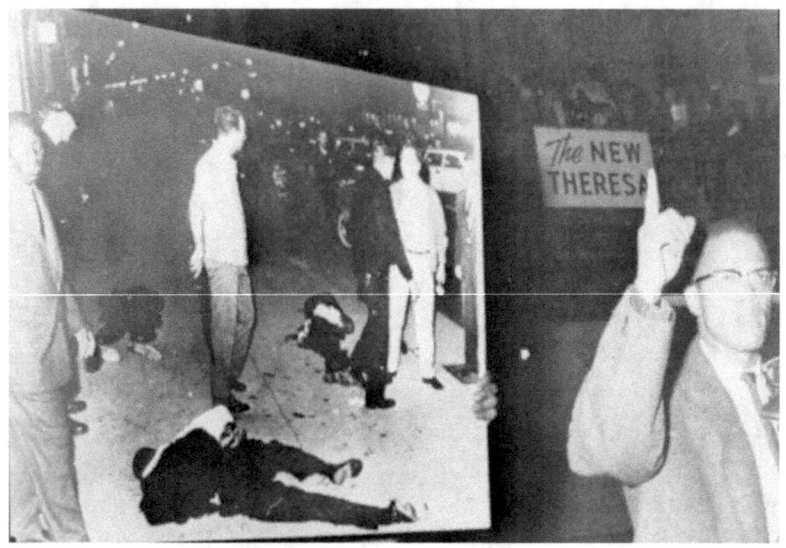

Malcom X. *Image courtesy of Documentary Photo Aids.*

☾

It is the duty of every Muslim to make a pilgrimage to Mecca at least once in their lifetime if they are physically and financially able to do so. After ending his association with Elijah Muhammed, Malcolm X fulfilled his obligation. It was the turning point of his life. As he journeyed to Mecca, Malcolm X was shocked to find that he was well known in the Muslim world. He was greeted enthusiastically wherever he went. In Mecca he met worshippers from all over the world. Much to his surprise some were White. He now learned that the teachings of the Prophet Mohammed did not condemn any individual for the color of his skin, rather a person was judged by his deeds. Malcolm X was now forced to reassess his thinking. He embraced the teachings of Orthodox Islam and returned to the United States a changed man.

Arriving back in the United States, Malcolm X's break with Elijah Muhammed and the Nation of Islam was now complete. His disaffection was no longer based solely on disenchantment with Muhammed's personal conduct. Now it was based on fundamental philosophical and spiritual differences. Malcolm X continued to attack racism and speak out on the importance of Black identity, but he no longer viewed the White man as the devil. In fact, he welcomed and encouraged Whites to work within their own groups to wipe out racism.

Malcolm X now attempted to establish an organization, which he called The Organization of African-American Unity. It was a particularly difficult task. His message was new, and many in the Black community were confused as to his purpose and goals. While Martin Luther King, Jr., focused on civil rights in America, Malcolm X was talking about human rights and looking to unite Black people around the world. He asked the United Nations to censure the United States for its racism. The heads of 33 independent African nations supported Malcolm X's censure proposal.

Malcolm X's philosophy appeared to be contradictory. He opposed Martin Luther King, Jr.'s movement of non-violence and integration. He would rail against the violence of White people and espouse the need for vigorous self-defense. On the other hand, Malcolm X would tell of his regret at rejecting a White college girl's offer to assist his organization and he would speak in support King's efforts for voter registration. All the while he was under constant attack from the Nation of Islam. The Black community did not rush to join Malcolm X's new organization.

On February 21, 1965, while appearing at the Audubon Theater in Harlem, Malcolm X was assassinated. There are conflicting theories about his assassination. Whether or not Malcolm X was killed on orders from Elijah Muhammed or as a result of a government conspiracy matters little today. As the years have passed, Malcolm X's stature has grown. His message of self-reliance, self-determination, pride in being Black, and appreciation of the African heritage and culture is better understood and accepted by all Americans, Black and White, than it was in 1965.

❮

In retrospect, the 1960s was one of the most turbulent decades in American history. This decade witnessed assassination of three national leaders and a war that was so divisive that fathers disowned their sons and a whole generation rejected their government. It was a time of social upheaval. Sex was now openly shared and even flaunted. Marijuana and psychedelic drug usage spread across the nation's campuses. Violent protests became routine. Amid this turmoil Black America embarked on its crusade for civil rights.

Little Rock had closed out the 1950s with a preview of the difficulties Blacks would experience in the 1960s. On February 1, 1960, the curtain rose. Four students—Joseph McNeil, Franklin McCain, David Richmond, and Ezell Blair, Jr.—sat at the lunch counter in the Woolworth's department store in Greensboro, North Carolina, and asked to be served. They were denied service and arrested for violating local segregation laws. Soon students across the South were following their example and demanding service in what became known as sit-ins. The sit-in was a very effective tactic. Students would fill every seat at a lunch counter and remain there until served. This prevented White customers from using the lunch counters. Business owners soon retaliated by having the local police evict the students. As soon as one group of students was evicted, a new group would take the seats of those who had been arrested. Faced with the passive resistance of the students, the police, the store owners and the public became increasingly frustrated. This frustration, combined with a general belief in Black inferiority and Jim Crow laws, more often than not resulted in violence against the students. By the following April, the protesting students had organized and formed a national organization called the Student Non-Violent Coordinating Committee (SNCC).

The sit-in in Nashville, Tennessee, in February 1960, was of particular importance. It was led by three students from Fisk University: John Lewis, Angela Butler, and Diane Nash.[68] The Fisk students had been

Students are conducting a 1962 *sit-in*. They are doing their homework at a Woolworth's lunch counter in Little Rock, Arkansas. *Image courtesy of Documentary Photo Aids.*

trained in non-violent tactics and were prepared for the worst. The first week of the protest was uneventful. The students occupied the lunch counter of a local store and did their homework. Then on February 27th, they were attacked by a group of Whites. The police did nothing to stop the attack. Eventually, the Black students were arrested, convicted of disorderly conduct, and fined. Many were put in jail for refusing to pay the fines. At this point the local Black community rallied on the students' behalf and boycotted White businesses that refused to serve Blacks.

On April 19, 1960, a bomb exploded at the home of one of Nashville's Black City Councilmen. Incredibly, no one was injured. This incident solidified the Black community and led to the first major march of the civil rights movement. The Black populace of Nashville marched through the city to the Mayor's office where they brought their protest directly to Mayor Ben West. Diane Nash confronted the mayor, asking him if he personally condoned discrimination. To his credit Mayor

West responded that he did not believe it morally right for a merchant to sell merchandise to a customer and then deny that customer service. Three weeks later the lunch counters of Nashville were fully integrated.

Martin Luther King, Jr.'s Southern Christian Leadership Conference (SCLC) and the Student Non-Violent Coordinating Committee (SNCC) were relatively new organizations and had not yet fully established credibility in the Black community or with the American public. In May 1961, another organization became active on the civil rights scene. The Congress of Racial Equality (CORE) decided to test how the South was complying with the integration orders of the Interstate Commerce Commission. Unlike SCLC and SNCC, CORE was an established organization, having been founded in 1942.

CORE organized groups of Blacks and Whites to board interstate buses and ride across the South. The purpose of these groups, called Freedom Riders, was to integrate interstate buses, terminals, lunch counters and rest rooms. The very nature of the Freedom Riders' mission and the composition of the individual groups made a violent reception at their destinations almost a certainty. In city after city they were beaten and attacked while the local police either took part or did nothing.

Although sit-ins were often confrontational, the violence directed at them paled in relation to that directed at the Freedom Riders. Southern Whites viewed the sit-ins as a local problem. It was a problem involving their own niggers and it could be handled. Whites reasoned that local Blacks knew if their protests went too far, they would be lynched. The Freedom Riders were different. They were outsiders, troublemakers. Some of the Freedom Riders were White—*nigger lovers* in the eyes of the locals.[69] Worse yet, some of the Whites were women. This was an incendiary combination that was bound to explode. And it did. On the outskirts of Anniston, Alabama, a firebomb was tossed into a crowded bus, destroying the bus and injuring many of the passengers.

The Freedom Riders won a major victory in 1962, when the Interstate Commerce Commission ordered that all seats on public transportation be available to everyone. It also ordered signs indicating *White* and *Colored* be removed. The Freedom Rider movement continued through 1963, but with mixed results. The public was repulsed by the violence that followed the Freedom Riders and concluded that the violence would stop if other means of achieving integration were explored.

Violence erupted again in the fall of 1962, when an Air Force veteran, James Meredith, attempted to enroll at the University of Mississippi. Mississippi had long been recognized as a hotbed of racism. Governor Ross Barnett was prepared to defy the federal government and resurrected the old Confederate issue of States Rights as a defense. He even appointed himself as Registrar of the University for the sole purpose of preventing Meredith's enrollment. When the federal government thwarted Barnett's efforts, a mob took matters into its own hands. The ensuing riot claimed two lives, wounded many others and required over twelve thousand federal troops to quell it. One of the dead was a French reporter. In his last dispatch Paul Guihard wrote, "The Civil War has never ended."[70] In his book, *Before The Mayflower* Lerone Bennett called this riot *The Mississippi Insurrection.*

The year 1963 should have been wonderful for Black and White America. It was the 100th anniversary of the Emancipation Proclamation, the "Year of the Jubilee." After 100 years the nation should have expected to celebrate a coming together of the races and to give thanks that the nation had survived a terrible civil war. Instead the year opened with troops patrolling the streets of Oxford, Mississippi, and would end with the assassination of President John F. Kennedy. In between would be confrontation in Birmingham, Alabama, the murder of the NAACP's Mississippi representative Medgar Evers, a massive march on Washington, and the bombing of a Sunday school that claimed the lives of four young Black girls. What should have been a joyous year was a terrible year.

❮

The year of 1963 was also a pivotal year in the quest for civil rights. There were more than 10,000 sit-ins and racial demonstrations. There were also riots in Cambridge, Maryland; Danville, Virginia; and Savannah, Georgia. More than 5,000 Black Americans were arrested for taking part in political activities. Ironically, in places like Little Rock and Oxford, where Whites had previously violently defied the federal government, very few arrests were made.

The eyes of the nation now focused on Birmingham, Alabama. Martin Luther King, Jr. recognized Birmingham as the most racist city in the United States. He believed that if he could successfully integrate that bastion of segregation his non-violent movement could succeed anywhere. In Birmingham, King and his associates embarked on a plan of confrontation they called *Project C.* Their goals included the integration of lunch counters, public drinking fountains, stores, rest rooms and other public facilities. They wanted to eliminate discriminatory hiring practices among local businesses and industries. They also wanted the city to establish a biracial committee to further the integration of the Black community into the life of the city.[71] For Dr. King there was an additional yet unspoken goal, to reestablish his credibility as leader of the civil rights movement.

In the fall of 1961, King had been asked by Dr. William G. Anderson to go to Albany, Georgia, and assist the efforts of a group called the Albany Movement to integrate public transportation facilities. King recognized that Albany was not a big enough stage to change the course of civil rights nationwide. Nevertheless, he reluctantly agreed. It was a mistake.

The Albany Movement consisted of several coalitions. The predominant group, SNCC, was more militant than King and resented his arrival on their turf. He remained in Albany only two days. Prior to leaving he, along with local politicians and law enforcement officials, held a press conference. They announced an agreement on specific issues. The agreements didn't last. King was criticized by the national press and by many Blacks for failing to achieve true integration in

Albany. Birmingham would provide an opportunity to regain his stature as the leader of the civil rights movement.

In Birmingham *Project C* would be based on four principles King had used so successfully in the past: exercise the right to vote; boycott businesses that practiced segregation; use the courts to protect civil rights; and participate in non-violent protest. But *Project C* had one additional element of dramatic symbolism. It was scheduled for the weeks leading up to Easter Sunday and would culminate during Holy Week. The struggle for civil rights led by a Black minister was intertwined with the events leading to the betrayal, crucifixion, and resurrection of Jesus Christ. It was spellbinding drama.

Opposing King was Police Commissioner Eugene "Bull" Connor. Connor looked every inch the part of the red-necked racist. He was a middle-aged man of medium height and average build. However, he exuded an animal quality of brute strength. When he spoke, he spoke forcefully without reservation and with a dedicated purpose. "Bull" Connor was clearly not a man to be tested. But that is exactly what King intended to do. Connor had a personal stake in the events that were about to take place. He wanted to be mayor of Birmingham, but he had just lost the election to his rival segregationist Albert Boutwell.[72] Connor was challenging the election in the courts when Martin Luther King, Jr. decided to challenge the segregation practices of the City of Birmingham.

On Wednesday April 3, 1963, *Project C* began with sit-ins and picketing of stores in Birmingham's business district. On Saturday, April 6th, the Reverend Fred Shuttlesworth of the Alabama Christian Conference led a small street demonstration. The following day, Palm Sunday, there was a larger demonstration that led to the first confrontation between the demonstrators and the police. The police easily dispersed the approximately 600 demonstrators.

The focus of the struggle now shifted to Birmingham's Kelly-Ingram Park. This park had one distinguishing characteristic. On one side stood the Sixteenth Street Baptist Church. While Dr. King used the

145

Gaston Motel as his command post, the Sixteenth Street Baptist Church served as the marshalling area for his demonstrators. It was from here that they would march through the park to challenge the authority of "Bull" Connor and the City of Birmingham. Connor had decided to prevent the demonstrations by stopping them in the park. Thus Kelly-Ingram Park became a familiar site to television audiences across the nation. What they saw was snarling police dogs and high-pressure fire hoses attacking defenseless demonstrators.

On April 12th Martin Luther King, Jr. defied a local judge's injunction barring protest marches. It was Good Friday and the Reverend King was arrested for exercising the rights granted to him in the U.S. Constitution. He would remain in jail for eight days. King's arrest was not a planned part of *Project C*. In fact it was more of a spontaneous act, resulting from frustration.[73] Up to this point the demonstrations were not going as well as King had hoped. The Black community was still divided about the demonstrations and King's presence had not been embraced by all. He felt he had to do something, anything, to jump-start the effort. And jump-start it he did with the unwitting help of eight White clergymen.

The Episcopal Bishop of Alabama, the Auxiliary Bishop of the Roman Catholic Church, and a leading Rabbi were among the eight clergymen who published a letter urging the Black community to withdraw its support of King and to work for change within the system. The letter attacked King as an outsider and troublemaker and was an appeal for the status quo.

Rather than achieve its purpose, the letter provided King with an opening to regain the support of the Black community. He countered with his now famous *Letter from a Birmingham Jail*. The letter was wrapped in spiritual analogies. He compared his mission of spreading the gospel of freedom in Birmingham to that of the Apostle Paul spreading the gospel of Jesus. He explained the necessity of non-violent protest and reassured the people of Birmingham that he was not going to go away or abandon the Black community.[74]

Dr. King had experienced jail before. In fact, he had been in jail 13 times. Nevertheless, being incarcerated in the Birmingham jail was unsettling. He knew that his life was in "Bull" Connor's hands. Had he wanted to Connor could easily have arranged for King to be killed attempting to escape. However, King also knew that every day he spent in jail drew national attention to the civil rights movement, and although he could easily have raised the $300 needed for bail, he chose to remain in jail. King's prolonged time in jail also had a negative side, however. Without its leader, the Birmingham demonstrations were being thwarted by the police and the movement was losing its impact.

When he was released from jail, Martin Luther King, Jr. faced his most difficult and dangerous decision. Jim Bevel, a King aide, proposed to use children in the demonstrations.[75] The idea was appealing. Children were available and willing to participate. They didn't face the pressures of having to hold a job, look after a family, or meet a mortgage payment so they were free to go to jail if arrested. Chasing after them would also be an embarrassment to "Bull" Connor and his helmeted policemen. It seemed like a perfect solution for energizing the demonstrations. But what if a child was killed? That was the question King faced. He chose to use the children and the results were dramatic.

❆

On May 2nd, the children streamed out of the Sixteenth Street Baptist Church and into Kelly-Ingram Park. They squirmed under the police barricades and, after avoiding capture, would reassemble to parade in the downtown. There they would allow themselves to be solemnly arrested and happily be carted off to fill the city's jails. If the situation hadn't been so serious, it would have had a carnival atmosphere.

Children or not, "Bull" Connor wasn't about to let the demonstrators get the upper hand. In the days that followed he augmented his police force and snarling dogs with firemen armed with high-pressure hoses. He was determined to wash away the problem.

147

In July 1963, firemen in Birmingham, Alabama used high pressure water hoses to disperse crowds of protesters. The sight of protesters, including children, being washed away sickened President Kennedy. Kennedy subsequently introduced legislation that eventually became the Civil Rights Act of 1964. *Image courtesy of Documentary Photo Aids.*

The sight of defenseless children being hit with a stream of water, pressurized at approximately 100 pounds per square inch, was not pretty. As scenes of Connor's men hosing down the demonstrators flashed on television screens across the country, a sense of revulsion swelled. President Kennedy later admitted the sight made him sick. In Birmingham, the sight of children being hosed united the Black community against the common enemy. Although he didn't yet know it, Connor had just lost the battle of Birmingham. Before a final truce could be reached, however, more scenes had yet to be played, some dangerous.

On Saturday, May 4th, an angry crowd assembled at the Sixteenth Street Baptist Church to begin a new march. This time angry adults joined the youths. Some were armed with switchblades while others were seen carrying guns. Even before the march had begun, rocks and other debris were being thrown from the rooftops around the square. A catastrophe was averted only by the quick actions of the Reverend Jim Bevel. Bevel grabbed a policeman's bullhorn and commanded those who were not prepared to follow the dictates of non-violence to leave. Fortunately, the crowd listened and soon dispersed. The following day Black couples entered 21 White churches for Sunday services. Only four were allowed to worship among the White congregations while the rest were turned away.

By now the events in Birmingham were international news as pictures of the children being hit with the pressurized water appeared in newspapers throughout the world. At this time the United States and the Soviet Union were locked in an ideological struggle known as the Cold War. The Soviet government newspaper, *Pravda*, gleefully ran a cartoon of a Birmingham policeman intimidating a child. America's image as the land of the free was being tarnished and members of Congress were now condemning the City of Birmingham. The Attorney General was calling for a truce. But nothing could change the mind or actions of "Bull" Connor or his partner in hate Alabama Governor George Wallace. In response to a reporter's question about world opinion of Alabama Wallace said: "The average man in Africa and Asia doesn't know where he is much less where Alabama is." [76]

With the adult Black community fully mobilized, there were more demonstrations, more confrontations, and more arrests. Before long the jails were full. The tension mounted and reached its climax when the Reverend Charles Billups, leading a crowd of demonstrators, came face to face with "Bull" Connor and his men, his dogs, and his hoses. The police demanded the group to stop. Billups urged them to continue marching in the name of the Lord. Connor gave the order to turn on the hoses. Billups dropped to his knees. Those behind him did likewise. They waited. Connor again commanded for the hoses to be turned on. Nothing happened as the White firemen looked from one to another. Then one fireman burst into tears and dropped his nozzle.

Others followed suit. The test of wills had been shattered. The march continued for a short while and then dispersed.

On Friday May 10, 1963, with the assistance of the Deputy United States Attorney General, an agreement was brokered between the City of Birmingham and its Black community. On that day Martin Luther King, Jr. announced that the agreement included:

- Desegregation of lunch counters, fitting rooms, rest rooms, and drinking fountains in all Birmingham stores within 90 days.
- Placement of Blacks in clerical and sales jobs in stores within 60 days.
- Release of prisoners still in jail on low bail.
- Establishment of permanent communication between Black and White leaders.[77]

The victory of the Black community was short lived. Robert Shelton and his Ku Klux Klan were quick to condemn the agreements. He claimed the agreements didn't speak for White people. He then made a veiled threat that it would not be healthy for Martin Luther King, Jr., to remain in Birmingham. Several hours later a bomb exploded at the Gaston Motel. Fortunately, King had already left for Atlanta. Later, Blacks protesting the bombing of the Gaston Motel were beaten by the Alabama State Police. A full-fledged riot followed. Riots then broke out in other cities and across the nation.

The events in Birmingham forced President Kennedy to take a more forceful stand on civil rights. Until then, Kennedy had been more supportive than his predecessors, but he hadn't truly been a civil rights activist. On June 11, ten hours after George Wallace had personally attempted to prevent two Black students from entering the University of Alabama, the President went on television and addressed the nation. He proposed new civil rights legislation and said it was time for Congress to act. The battle of Birmingham had finally brought the full force of the Presidency into the civil rights movement. Shortly after midnight the President's plea was answered with a bullet. Medgar Evers was assassinated.

❰

During the civil rights movement Martin Luther King, Jr., Ralph Abernathy, Andrew Young, and other leaders appeared at demonstrations across the country. Celebrities such as singer Harry Belafonte and comedian Dick Gregory also made appearances. Medgar W. Evers was the field secretary for the NAACP in Mississippi. What separated Evers from the other leaders was that he lived in Mississippi. Once a demonstration or confrontation ended the celebrities and national leaders would leave the area and prepare for their next effort. Local leaders, like Evers, remained behind to face the problems that were still unresolved. This made them particular targets of the hate mongers.

Medgar Evers was a combat veteran of World War II. He had been a leading player in the efforts to integrate the University of Mississippi. Later, he led the fight to desegregate public facilities in Jackson, Mississippi. It was not an easy time. More than 700 demonstrators had been jailed, including Roy Wilkins, the National Secretary of the NAACP. About 15 minutes after midnight on the morning of June 12, 1963, Medgar Evers drove into his driveway. He was glad to be home after a difficult day. As he stepped out of his car, a single shot rang out and Evers fell to the ground. By the time his wife and children reached him, he was dead.

Investigators found a high powered rifle in the bushes near Evers' home. They traced it to Byron De La Beckwith, a known White supremacist. Beckwith's fingerprint was allegedly found on the rifle's telescopic sight. He was charged with the murder of Medgar Evers. After two all-White and all-male juries were unable to reach a verdict, the case was dropped without resolution in 1969. Twenty-three years later the case was re-opened, based on new evidence, and an unrepentant Byron De La Beckwith was convicted of the murder of Medgar Evers.[78] For Mrs. Myrlie Evers the conviction of Beckwith was the culmination of years of prayers. She then began a new chapter in her life when she was elected chairman of the NAACP in 1994.

❮

Martin Luther King, Jr., knew that it was one thing for President Kennedy to propose legislation to the Congress. Successfully turning the proposal into law was another matter. Although the President was in his corner, King knew that history was not. Civil rights legislation had almost always failed in the past. Southern Congressmen were skilled at the intricacies of vote counting. A promise here, a vote there had been successful in thwarting past efforts. Then, too, if all else failed, they could always fall back on the filibuster. However, after Birmingham, the powerful voice of public opinion was calling for action. King's task was to harness that public opinion and create a force that would overwhelm the tactics of the Southerners. He settled for a massive demonstration in the nation's capital. It would forever be known as the March on Washington, the defining moment of King's public life.

The idea of a massive march on the nation's capital had been the dream of Asa Phillip Randolph for a long, long time. At the beginning of World War II, he had threatened President Franklin Roosevelt that he would bring 100,000 Black men and women to Washington to protest job discrimination. An irritated, but not disbelieving, Roosevelt dissuaded Randolph with a Presidential Executive Order barring discrimination in the defense industries. Now in 1963, the 100th anniversary of the Emancipation Proclamation, Randolph argued that the logical follow up to the events in Birmingham was a massive march demanding passage of the President's proposed civil rights legislation. The leaders of the NAACP, CORE, SNCC, the Urban League and others agreed with him. All thought the idea appealing. Each had his own vision of the march, but Randolph forcefully maintained control of the planning. If nothing else he insisted the march would be dignified. The one dissenter was Malcolm X. Malcolm X would later refer to the demonstration as "The Farce on Washington."

The idea of a massive march on Washington by thousands of Black men terrified John F. Kennedy. He could see the streets of Washington blocked and the halls of Congress filled with Black protesters. Violence, in his mind, was unavoidable. He believed the proposed march threatened any hope he had for passage of his civil rights legislation. President Kennedy, his brother the Attorney General, Vice President Lyndon Johnson, and other members of the administration met with Randolph, King, Roy Wilkins, and others at the White House on Saturday June 22nd. The discussions were not unpleasant, but the atmosphere was one of determination. The President wanted the march called off. The civil rights leaders refused. The march would take place on August 28th.

Following the White House meeting the civil rights leaders, particularly Dr. King, crossed the country making appearances and speeches in support of the march. By the time President Kennedy returned from a scheduled European trip, the idea for the march had taken on a new momentum. White and Black organizations were lending their support. By August 1st, approximately $100,000 had been raised. An organization of Black New York City police officers had volunteered 2,000 of its members to act as crowd control.[79] President Kennedy now saw that, unless he acted quickly, the administration would be left out of what now appeared to be an important event. He then invited the civil rights leaders to another White House meeting and endorsed the march. Nevertheless, a nagging fear of potential violence lurked beneath the surface.

Within the civil rights group there were fears as well. Now that the march had the President's endorsement, Randolph believed it was particularly important to ensure a dignified gathering and not to offend or embarrass Kennedy. In outlining the day's activities, Randolph had not assigned specific topics to the various speakers. However, he had limited each speech to a maximum of eight minutes. On the night before the march John Lewis of SNCC released a copy of his remarks to the press causing a crisis within the civil rights leadership. The remarks included a statement critical of the Kennedy administration. On learning what Lewis planned to say, the Roman Catholic Archbishop of Washington, Patrick O'Boyle, took offense. O'Boyle was scheduled to give the convocation to open the march. Now he telephoned Randolph and refused to participate. Randolph persuaded Lewis to change his remarks and O'Boyle stayed on the program.

On the day of the march, people came from all corners of the nation, some 250,000 strong. About one-fourth of them were White. They began gathering at the Washington monument as early as 1:00AM. The plan was for the group to be entertained first at the Washington monument and then march in unison to the Lincoln Memorial. Plans, however, don't always go as scheduled, and by noon the crowds had gathered along the Reflecting Pool all the way to the Lincoln Memorial. President Kennedy needn't have worried. This crowd was a happy crowd. They mingled and walked along the streets of Washington as they drifted toward the Lincoln Memorial. Crowd control was impossible but unnecessary. The day was a typical hot summer day, but there was electricity in the air that replaced the otherwise sultry humidity.

At the Lincoln Memorial Joan Baez, Mahalia Jackson, and Peter, Paul, and Mary entertained. Sammy Davis Jr., Dr. Ralph Bunche, Lena Horne, and Jackie Robinson were warmly received with cheers and shouts as each in turn was recognized. Then A. Phillip Randolph, dignified as ever, introduced the speakers.

Martin Luther King, Jr., was scheduled to be the last speaker. As he sat on the platform listening, he calculated that it would be close to three o'clock before he spoke. He worried that the crowd would have had enough sun and speeches by then and many would leave. Worse, he could see that those speaking before him had touched on almost every point he planned to make.

Dr. King had worked hard on his speech. He had been up until the early hours revising and refining each word. He liked to use analogies in his speeches. For this speech he had chosen the image of a bad check. Abraham Lincoln had issued the check in the Emancipation Proclamation, but now 100 years later it still had not been redeemed. This was the theme he planned to use. For a moment he considered using an image about his dreams. He had used it earlier in a speech in Detroit but decided against it for this Washington speech. King knew that he was more effective and impassioned when he spoke extemporaneously so he worked extra hard to make this important speech something to remember.[80]

As the day wore on King's fears began to materialize. The heat and humidity were winning the battle for the crowd. People were beginning to look for a cooler place. Then King was introduced. For a moment there was silence. Then the crowd roared their welcome and approval for the man who had beaten the segregationists in Birmingham. It was an electrifying moment, the type of moment that engulfs a person. It engulfed King, and he began to speak not from his notes but from his heart:

"I have a dream that one day this nation will rise up and live out the true meaning of its creed: 'We hold these truths to be self evident; that all men are created equal.'"

He spoke for only about ten minutes, but in that time he expressed his hope that his children and the children of all Americans would enjoy the freedoms promised in the Constitution. He concluded with the hope that all people—Black, White, Gentile or Jew—would reach a time when they could say together the words of the old Negro spiritual "Free at last! Free at last! Thank God Almighty we are free at last."

That afternoon Martin Luther King, Jr. said what many thought but were afraid to say. When would the United States of America practice what it preached? The crowd roared its approval, and in homes across the nation thoughtful men and women listened intently. Some were uncomfortable. Others, predictably, dismissed King's remarks as the ranting of a "pompous nigger." Most embraced his words.

When Dr. King left the stage, the ovation in response to his remarks was still ringing across the Mall. Whites and Blacks joined hands and sang the theme song of the civil rights movement, "We Shall Overcome." Then as if on cue, 200,000 people quietly went home. There was no riot. There was no demonstration in the halls of Congress. The only evidence of what had just occurred was the sight of the workmen picking up chairs, signs and the normal litter associated with any large gathering. The march was over. President Kennedy was elated and within minutes issued a statement to the press praising the day's activities.

‹

Not everyone was elated. Three weeks later on a bright fall morning, September 15, 1963, three fourteen-year-old girls, Cynthia Wesley, Carol Robertson, Addie Mae Collins, and their eleven-year-old friend Denise McNair were attending Sunday school at the Sixteenth Street Baptist Church in Birmingham. That day was the first of what was planned to be a monthly youth day service. Pastor John Cross had been concerned about lagging attendance by the young people of the parish.

Denise and Addie Mae were in the basement of the church waiting for the service to begin. They had gone to the ladies' lounge. Addie's sister Sarah was getting a drink of water when Denise asked Addie to tie her belt. They went over to the window for better light. Then Sarah saw a bomb come through the window and explode next to Addie and Denise.

Reverend Cross was upstairs when the bomb went off. By the time he reached the basement, Addie and Denise were dead. So were Cynthia Wesley and Carol Robertson. Sarah Collins survived but lost an eye. Twenty-two others were injured by the blast. As the ambulances and hearses cared for the dead and wounded, a rage ignited in the Black community and riots soon followed. For many people the concept of non-violent protest died that day.

Although the church was soon repaired, the pain of that awful day lingered. It was eight months before Reverend Cross held services again in the Sixteenth Street Baptist Church. It took 14 years for the bomber to be brought to justice. On November 17, 1977, Denise McNair's birthday, a White supremacist named R. M. Chambliss was convicted and sentenced to life in prison.

The apprehension, arrest, and conviction of Chambliss fulfilled a promise made by a young White man shortly after the four girls' funerals. Then a law student at the University of Alabama, Bill Baxley wrote the names of the young girls on a piece of paper and vowed that somehow justice would be served for their murders. He was elected Alabama Attorney General in 1971 and immediately re-opened the case. He met with obstructions at every turn. For example, it took him four years to gain access to the FBI files on the case. He did, however, receive help from an unexpected source. George Wallace, again Governor of Alabama, was undergoing a transition from intense racist to a man asking forgiveness. Wallace assisted Baxley by increasing his budget and putting the state's jet plane at his disposal. In time Baxley and his chief assistant Bob Eddy found witnesses who agreed to testify.[81]

☾

President Kennedy opened the year of 1963 with a special message to the Congress for the 100th anniversary of the Emancipation Proclamation. In it he pointedly remarked that regardless of where a Black baby was born in the United States that its opportunity for education, employment, and a full life was half that of a White baby born on the same day. His message was encouraging to the Black community. They felt that at last there was someone in the White House who understood and cared what happened to them. Kennedy's reaction to Birmingham, the murder of Medgar Evers, and the killing of the four little girls further bolstered Blacks' belief that here was a man who would help them. On November 22nd, their hopes shattered along with the rest of America. The President was assassinated in Dallas, Texas.

Black America looked to the future with uncertainty. Their champion was dead, and the man who replaced him was a Southerner. Lyndon Baines Johnson was a native of Texas. However, on closer inspection, he was a man with a long history of supporting civil rights. Almost his first act as the new President was to call for Congress to pass President Kennedy's civil rights legislation. He signed the Civil Rights

Act of 1964 on July 2nd. The act guaranteed access to public accommodations: restaurants, hotels, and amusement areas. It authorized the government to sue for the desegregation of schools and other facilities. Finally, it required equal employment and non-discrimination in federal programs.

❮

The English people have a saying in periods of difficult transition: "The King is dead, long live the King." In 1964, America, grieving at the loss of its dead President, crowned a new champion. His name was Cassius Clay, and in February 1964, he defeated Sonny Liston to become the heavyweight boxing champion of the world. Clay's victory was not universally welcomed. He was by any standards a brash, outspoken egotist whose antics were greeted with laughter and derision. His primary asset was that he had defeated a man who scared most of the public, an ex-con named Liston.

When Cassius Clay was 12 years old, somebody stole his bicycle. While reporting the incident to a local policeman, Bill Martin, an angry Cassius threatened to beat up the culprit. Martin took one look at the 78-pound Clay and suggested he join a local gym where Martin gave boxing instruction. Within six years, Clay learned his lessons so well that he won a gold medal at the 1960 Olympics in Rome. He then embarked on a professional boxing career that would lead him to the world championship. Along the way he also embraced the Muslim religion. Following his victory over Sonny Liston, Clay changed his name to Muhammad Ali. At the time he said that the name Clay was given to his family by slave masters and was an unworthy name for the world champion.

Muhammad Ali repeatedly defended his championship in the 1960s and was generally regarded as one of the best, if not the best, heavyweight champions of all time. However, in 1967, the Vietnam War did what no fighter had been able to accomplish. Ali's draft board scheduled him for induction into the armed forces. Ali refused on religious grounds and took his case to court. It would be 43 months before the Supreme Court upheld Ali's position. During that period, however, he was stripped of his title and denied the opportunity to fight. Instead he accepted invitations to speak on college campuses where he reaffirmed his religious convictions against killing and in the process won a wide number of admirers, Black and White.

In October 1970, Ali resumed his boxing career and regained his title in 1974 by defeating George Foreman. After successfully defending his title in October 1975, in a thrilling fight with Joe Frazier, an overconfident Ali lost the title to Leon Spinks on February 15, 1978. Seven months later Ali did what no other fighter had done; he won the heavyweight championship for the third time by defeating Spinks in a rematch. Ali's boxing career came to a close when he lost the title to his former sparring partner, Larry Holmes, on October 2, 1980.

Muhammad Ali completed the bridge between Black and White America that had been started by Joe Louis. Louis was not a controversial champion. He was admired and even loved. In later years he was pitied. Ali, on the other hand, was an unavoidable tornado. He was the self-proclaimed greatest fighter of all time and by the end of his career few doubted it. However, he was also a man of conviction and a humanitarian who struck a chord with America. He was a man to be admired who happened to be Black. Without Ali, Michael Jordan would not be an icon today. Thirty-six years after winning the gold medal in Rome, Muhammad Ali lit the torch that opened the 1996 Olympic Games in Atlanta. Americans of every hue cheered their hero.

❮

With the murder of the four girls in Birmingham the non-violent philosophy of Martin Luther King, Jr. was challenged in Black America. Young firebrands like Stokeley Carmichael and H. Rap Brown were calling for more direct confrontation. Malcolm X was espousing his famous line "by any means necessary." Also there was a change in the composition of the protesters. Until then most of the protests had been confined to the South, and those involved were quasi-professional pro- testers trained in the tactics of non-violence. Now the discontent had spread north and included new groups: Korean War veterans, working class Blacks, and the disadvantaged. Not surprisingly, on July 18, 1964, a riot broke out in Harlem that left one person dead, over one hundred injured, and many more arrested.

In response to civil disturbances and national unrest President Johnson initiated a series of programs known as the War on Poverty and created the Office of Economic Opportunity. The War on Poverty never had a chance. It was immediately mired in the differing interests of national and local politicians and for all its well-meaning goals was ineffective. One program in the War on Poverty, *Project 100,000*, was to have a devastating impact on the Black community in a real war that would soon be fought in a place called Vietnam.

Project 100,000 was designed to take one hundred thousand poor, illiterate individuals off the streets and place them into the military. The idea was to expose these individuals to the discipline of recruit training, and to provide a place for them to live, earn money, and improve their life opportunities. While in the service these individuals would be given a basic education in reading, writing, and mathematics in addition to their military instruction. Six months prior to the end of their two-year enlistment, they would be assigned to another program called *Project Transition*. Here they would be taught skills that would be marketable in civilian life: mechanic, press operator, bulldozer opera- tor, etc. At the completion of this training they would be discharged from the service with money in their pockets and equipped to function as a useful member of society. On paper it was a noble effort. The tragedy was that when hostilities broke out in Vietnam, the military's need for manpower and money escalated dramatically. Recruiters still scoured the inner cities for *Project 100,000* prospects, but *Project Transi- tion* went by the wayside. Unable to qualify for jobs demanding com- plex educational skills, the inner city recruits were assigned to the in-

fantry, artillery, motor transport, and tank units. These units were traditionally in more direct contact with the enemy, and thus Black casualties were disproportionately high.

The Civil Rights Act of 1964, signed by Lyndon Johnson on July 2nd,
had no provision for enforcing voting rights. That battle was yet to be
won, and it had begun earlier that year in Mississippi with tragic results.
The late Medgar Evers and the NAACP had been working hard to
encourage Blacks to register to vote. Registering to vote, a routine chore
for a Northern White, was a dangerous proposition for a Mississippi
Black. Blacks who attempted to register were intimidated and in some
cases murdered. In the spring of 1964, the Student Non-Violent Coordinating Committee (SNCC) initiated a voter registration drive in
Mississippi. They brought in student workers, White and Black, from
across the country. SNCC reasoned that the students would be safe.
Their parents were from all walks of life and many were affluent Whites.
Surely, no one would dare harm these students.

Andrew Goodman was 20 years old when he arrived in Mississippi.
He was White and from New York City. His companions were two
workers from the Congress of Racial Equality (CORE). James Chaney,
age 21, was Black. Michael Schwerner, age 24, was White. On June 21,
Andrew Goodman's first day in Mississippi, the three drove out to
investigate the burning of a Black church. The church had been the site
of a civil rights meeting three weeks earlier. At approximately 3:00PM, in
the town of Philadelphia, they were stopped for speeding by Deputy
Sheriff Cecil Price. The three were taken to the police station and de-
tained until about 10:30PM when they were released. Then they disap-
peared. The whereabouts of Goodman, Chaney, and Schwerner soon
became a national issue. The local sheriff, Lawrence Rainet, made little
effort to locate the three missing civil rights workers. Eventually, President Johnson ordered 200 unarmed sailors to the area to assist the FBI
in conducting a search. They found nothing there.

On August 4th the bodies of Goodman, Chaney, and Schwerner
were found in a mud dam that was used to create a watering hole for

cattle on a nearby farm. Each of the men had been shot. However, Chaney, the only Black, had obviously been severely beaten as well. The FBI located the bodies with the aid of an informant who implicated 21 local residents in the killing. Despite obtaining a confession from one individual that the killing of the three men was a Ku Klux Klan plot, the charges against the men were dismissed.

Eventually, Deputy Sheriff Price and six others were convicted in a federal court of violating the three men's civil rights and given sentences ranging from three to ten years. Years later the story of Andrew Goodman, James Chaney, and Michael Schwerner was portrayed in the movie *Mississippi Burning*, starring Gene Hackman.

The tumultuous year of 1964 came to a close on a happy note. On December 10th, in Oslo, Norway, Dr. Martin Luther King, Jr. was awarded the Nobel Peace Prize. He was the first African American and the youngest person to receive this prestigious award.

☾

The voting rights issue was not confined to Mississippi. SNCC operatives had been working in the area of Dallas County, Alabama, throughout the summer of 1964. Then in January 1965, the voting rights issue came to an explosive head in a small town called Selma. One hundred years earlier the people of Selma, Alabama had watched as blue-coated Union soldiers occupied their town. Now they watched with alarm as Black activists began threatening their way of life. It didn't take an accountant to realize if the Blacks were allowed to vote they would by their sheer numbers take over the political, economic, and educational systems. Worse yet was the prospect of Blacks dominating the social life of the town.

Change is rarely clean and simple. It is usually accompanied by fear, real or imagined. Such was the case in Selma. Nevertheless, there were within the White establishment conciliatory voices willing to consider accepting change. Among them were some members of the business community and, surprisingly, the local Chief of Police, Wilson Baker. However, the forces of fear and bigotry, personified by Dallas County's Sheriff Jim Clark, drowned out reason and confrontation was inevitable.

There was discord within the civil rights groups as well. By the time Martin Luther King, Jr. arrived in Selma, SNCC had been working in the community for over a year. SNCC resented King's intrusion and his penchant for making an appearance, generating enthusiasm and publicity, and then leaving for another mission. In addition, SNCC was not as committed to non-violence as Dr. King and his associates. Nevertheless, he had a national reputation and a Nobel Peace Prize. It was hard to ignore him.

Dr. King employed a familiar strategy in Selma. He planned to use civil disobedience to fill the jails and cause such a disruption that the authorities would be forced to negotiate. However, he soon learned that the will of a small town that believes it is fighting for its existence is not so easily broken. Throughout January and February 1965, Sheriff Jim Clark met Black attempts at voter registration with increasing violence. Clark had a penchant for clubbing anyone who protested or attempted to thwart him. It made little difference to him if the object of his wrath was a young girl or a man of the cloth. He treated them equally. He clubbed them.

In March, after failing to get assistance from President Lyndon Johnson, King decided on a broader strategy. He announced he would lead a march to the state capitol at Montgomery and appeal to Governor George Wallace and the Alabama Legislature. The Governor's response was to issue an order prohibiting the march. He then sent state troopers, commanded by Colonel Al Lingo, to reinforce Sheriff Clark and prevent the march.

On Sunday March 7th, the White population of Selma eagerly anticipated the fate of the Blacks should they march. In another part of the city John Lewis and Hosea Williams of SNCC were knocking on doors trying to round up sufficient marchers. Lewis and Williams would lead the march that day. There had been a threat on King's life and all concerned agreed it would be better for him not to march. Understandably, there was some reluctance among the Black community to go out and march when there was a strong possibility that they would be beaten or killed. By late morning, Williams and Lewis had assembled approximately 500 marchers and soon they were headed down Sylvan Street toward the outskirts of town. Whites lined the street shouting and swearing every imaginable epithet.

When the marchers reached the Edmund Pettus Bridge, Sheriff Clark and his deputies, armed with cattle prods, stepped aside and let the marchers pass. At the top of the bridge, Colonel Lingo and his state troopers blocked their path. The troopers were armed with night sticks and tear gas. Some were mounted and carried whips. For a moment both sides hesitated and then Lingo ordered his men forward. Within minutes the situation was out of control. Troopers were beating and whipping marchers. Spectators were urging the troopers to "kill the niggers."

It was over in five minutes. Sixteen blacks were seriously injured. More than 40 others required medical treatment. John Lewis had a fractured skull. That night he vented his frustration and anger at a gathering at Brown's chapel. He wanted to know how President Johnson could send troops to Vietnam and not to Selma. Ten days later the Third Battalion of the Ninth Marine Regiment landed at Danang, Vietnam. Lewis and his compatriots were still left to fend for themselves.

Colonel Al Lingo and Sheriff Jim Clark did in Selma what "Bull" Connor did in Birmingham. They galvanized the nation behind the civil rights movement. The sight of defenseless marchers being whipped, trampled by horses, fired upon with tear gas, and shocked with electric cattle prods shamed the nation and sickened people worldwide.

Martin Luther King, Jr. vowed to lead a second march the following Tuesday. When word spread of his intentions, President Johnson sent an emissary to dissuade King. He was unsuccessful. Then the former governor of Florida, LeRoy Collins, contacted King and offered to broker a deal between King, Sheriff Clark, and Colonel Lingo that would prevent bloodshed on the second march. The agreement reached was that the marchers would cross the Pettus Bridge and then turn back before leaving the city limits. This allowed the government to say the demonstration had been confined to the city limits and King to say the marchers had successfully crossed the bridge. From the point of view of preventing violence the agreement was successful. The marchers crossed the bridge, the troopers took no action, and on King's order the marchers returned to Selma. However, King had deceived the marchers. He told them he would lead them to Montgomery that day. He had not told them that he had made a deal with Clark and Lingo. When he later had to admit publicly that he never intended to march to Montgomery that Tuesday, King lost considerable stature with the various civil rights groups: CORE, NAACP, SNCC, etc.[82]

The agreement between King, Clark, and Lingo did not protect the Reverend James Reed, a White Unitarian minister. After the second march Reed and two other White ministers ate dinner in a Black restaurant. When they left the restaurant, four Whites attacked them. Reed was struck on the head by a 2x4 board. He died later that night. The following morning a group of nuns and priests from Chicago who had participated in the second march rioted in the streets of Selma in protest of Reed's killing.

President Johnson went before the Congress and demanded passage of his voting rights bill. He knew the country was solidly behind him. As a Southerner he also knew the impact of his words when he said it was the responsibility of all Americans to overcome bigotry. He concluded his address to the Congress with the words from the civil rights theme song, *We Shall Overcome.*

There was a third and final March from Selma to Montgomery. This time the marchers were protected by federal troops. On the night before the triumphant march into Montgomery, the marchers were entertained by Harry Belafonte, Leonard Bernstein, Billy Eckstine, and Sammy Davis, Jr. The following day, 200,000 marchers walked past the Dexter Avenue Baptist church, where Martin Luther King, Jr. had begun his ministry, on to the steps of the state capitol. There they heard Dr. King say to the State of Alabama "We ain't gonna let nobody turn us around!"

The elation of the triumphant march into Montgomery was short lived. Viola Liuzzo was a White housewife from Detroit. Like many Northern Whites she was concerned about what was happening to Blacks in the South. She had gone to Selma to help. Her husband had supported her decision, but they had both agreed that she would not march. Her job was to drive marchers back to Selma after the march was over. Her guide was a nineteen-year-old Black man named Leroy Moton. Having delivered their first passengers to Selma, Viola and Leroy started on the return trip to Montgomery. Along the way, their car was overtaken by another carrying four members of the Ku Klux Klan. One of the Klansmen fired two shots from a .38 caliber pistol into the driver's window killing Viola Liuzzo. Once again America shuddered with shock.

President Lyndon Johnson signed the Voting Rights Act of 1965 on August 6. The Act authorized the President to send federal examiners into the South to register voters. Equally important, it prevented literacy tests from being used as criteria for voter qualification. Southern registrars could no longer require Blacks to answer unanswerable questions in order to register. With the stroke of the Presidential pen, the sacrifices of Birmingham and Selma, of Cynthia Wesley, Carol Robertson, Addie Mae Collins, Denise McNair, Andrew Goodman, James Chaney, Michael Schwerner, and Viola Luizzo were not in vain.

❮

After passage of the Voting Rights Act and prior to the formal signing ceremony, President Johnson delivered the commencement address to the graduating class at Howard University. Howard is a predominantly Black university on the outskirts of the nation's capital named for the former head of the Freedman's Bureau, General O. O. Howard.

It was a fitting setting for Johnson to trumpet the achievement of passing the Voting Rights Act. The President's remarks, however, went beyond anything the audience expected and set the stage for what became the most divisive issue of the next three decades.

Johnson argued that passage of the Voting Rights Act was not enough to rectify the disparity in the lifestyles of Blacks and Whites. He said that courts and the Congress had not been able to stem the economic gulf between the two races. He cited statistics that showed Black opportunities for jobs, life expectancy, housing and education were far inferior to those of Whites. He expressed concern that the cities would become isolated areas of Black poverty. To drive his point home, Johnson used the analogy of a track race. He said: "You do not take a person who for years has been hobbled by chains and liberate him, take him to the starting line, and say 'You are free to compete . . .' and still justly feel you have been completely fair." He concluded that more needed to be done to level the playing field. From this speech the concept of Affirmative Action emerged.[83]

In September 1965, President Johnson took steps to level the playing field. He issued Executive Order 11246 that required federal contractors "to take affirmative action to ensure that applicants are employed without regard to their race, creed, or national origin." Affirmative Action in Johnson's mind meant more than the elimination of outright discrimination. He wanted employers to seek out qualified applicants and inform the public of job opportunities. It was the spirit of the law that was important. Unfortunately, the spirit of the law was obscured by the requirement for major contractors, with more than 50 employees, to submit to the federal government a written program showing how they were complying with the new Executive Order. Soon Johnson's concept of providing a balanced playing field was lost and the term Affirmative Action became synonymous with Black favoritism.

❨

President Johnson's call for Affirmative Action had barely left his lips when proof of his insight exploded in Los Angeles, California, the City of Angels. It began on August 11, 1965, with a routine traffic violation. Marquette Frye, a Black unemployed worker, and his brother Ronald were driving 50 miles per hour in a 30 miles per hour zone in that part of Los Angeles known as Watts. He was drunk. Motorcycle policeman Lee W. Minkus, who was White, pulled Frye over and began the routine associated with a drunk driving citation. A crowd gathered to watch the proceedings. Initially the crowd was friendly, laughing at Marquette's drunken condition.

At first the alcohol let Frye view the situation as humorous as well, but later his laughter turned to fear as he recalled previous experiences with the law. He began to resist. Then his mother arrived on the scene and began shouting at Frye and the policeman. Officer Minkus sensed a change in the mood of the crowd and called for back-up. As more police arrived the crowd became larger and more unruly. It was only a matter of time before the incendiary combination of misunderstanding, frustration, poverty, and old resentments toward the police ignited into a full-scale riot.

For the next six days the Black community of Watts battled the full force of the White establishment. When it was over, 35 people were dead, 883 were injured, and more than 3,000 were jailed. Property damage was estimated at approximately $222 million. Subsequently, a commission headed by former CIA director John McCone investigated the causes of the riot. The McCone Commission concluded that the divisions between the Black and White communities were so severe that the riots in Watts were most likely a precursor of things to come. The report proved to be prophetic as 1966 saw riots in Cleveland, Brooklyn, Chicago, Omaha, and Dayton.

Scenes of the Watts riot filled television screens across the nation. Looters were everywhere: in grocery stores, appliance stores, and liquor stores. More ominous, looters were breaking into sporting goods stores and arming themselves. Stones, the traditional weapons of rioters, were replaced with rifles and handguns. When the police were augmented by 13,000 National Guardsmen, the scenes from Watts more closely resembled scenes from World War II than previous domestic riots.

The elected leadership of Los Angeles and the leadership within the Watts community were ineffective during the riot. At the height of hostilities, comedian Dick Gregory tried to calm the passions. He carried a bullhorn and walked the streets urging the people to go home. The crowd taunted him. A shot rang out. Gregory was hit in the leg. He continued to walk into the crowd, urging them to disperse. Admiring his bravery, some did. Then Gregory left for a hospital. Later, after the riot had subsided, Martin Luther King, Jr. walked the devastated streets seeking to console and heal. On one street he approached a group of young boys and introduced himself. He was surprised when one youngster responded "We won." Looking at the surrounding debris King asked the boy how he could believe that he had won. The boy replied "because we made them pay attention to us."[84] The fears, frustrations, and inequities in Black America that Lyndon Johnson described to the graduating class of Howard University were found in the smoldering chaos of Watts.

Unlike riots before and after, the Watts riot added a new phrase to American speech: "Burn, Baby, Burn." The phrase originated with a Los Angeles disc jockey called Magnificent Montague.[85] His show was so popular in Watts that it was almost required listening. He talked the language of the street. His chatter between songs included a phrase that had no particular meaning "Yahoo . . . burn, baby, burn." It was cool and teenagers in particular adopted it as a catch-all phrase. After August 11th, the phrase took on new meaning. As flames spread throughout Watts, "Burn, Baby, Burn" became the defiant chant of the mob. It meant more than simply burning buildings, cars, or any other flammable object. It was a message to White police and the leadership of Los Angeles to stay out of Watts. Later as riots spread across the nation, it became a message to White America of Black frustration and anger. It also became a slogan that was misunderstood and feared by Whites.

In retrospect 1965 was a turning point in the history of Black and White America. In March, President Johnson ordered U.S. Marines to land at Danang, Vietnam, and embarked on a war that would divide the country and topple the President. For Black Americans, Vietnam was a war that claimed the lives of a disproportionate number of their sons and spawned racial hatred. In August, the Voting Rights Act was signed. Shortly thereafter there were riots across the land. Perhaps more importantly, the struggle for civil rights now took a new turn. Martin Luther King, Jr.'s message of non-violence was being challenged by younger leaders. Stokely Carmichael had assumed leadership of SNCC and Floyd McKissic headed CORE. These men were impatient and frustrated. For them non-violence had not achieved results. King himself was beginning to go in a new direction. His previous efforts had been focused on the South. Now he was ready to focus his concern on the plight of Blacks in the North.

As the United States got more deeply involved in Vietnam, King saw a role for himself and SCLC on a larger stage. His desire to expand the role of SCLC was not shared by others within the organization. Nevertheless, in May 1965, King publicly opposed the war in Vietnam. In an August speech he said he would appeal directly to President Johnson and Ho Chi Minh for a negotiated settlement of the conflict. He earned the cheers of the crowd that day, but he lost the best friend he had for the civil rights movement. Lyndon Johnson was not a man to accept criticism graciously. King's venture into foreign policy also lost him support in the White community. Once he stepped beyond the field of civil rights, Whites who were previously willing to support him now viewed King as an "uppity nigger."

King's traditional allies were increasingly concerned that his foray into national politics would hurt the civil rights movement. They could already feel the alienation of Lyndon Johnson. They sensed the loss of White support as the country struggled with the issue of Vietnam. Roy Wilkins of the NAACP and Ralph Bunche, the former Ambassador to the United Nations and Nobel Peace Prize winner, were now saying that

Black Panthers march in Oakland, California in 1966. *Image courtesy of Documentary Photo Aids.*

King should assume one role or the other, but not both.

On the other side, those opposed to King's non-violent policies, Stokely Carmichael, the Nation of Islam, and the newly formed Black Panther Party were preaching a gospel of self-determination. They called it Black Power. This philosophy rejected integration and reliance on the White power structure. It emphasized pride in self and economic and social independence. It embraced self-determination and self-defense.[86] It was seen in the faces of young Black men and women wearing Black jackets, Black berets, and carrying a flag emblazoned with the image of a Black Panther. Black Power scared White America.

☾

The cold winds of January 1966 found Martin Luther King, Jr. with his eye trained on the city of Chicago. Earlier, he had viewed Birmingham as a key to opening the doors of the South. He looked at Chicago as the key to opening the rest of the nation. However, there were formidable obstacles to overcome not the least of which were Dr. King's unfamiliarity with the city, the apathy of its Black population, and the lack of a clear objective to attack. He would spend the next seven months working the city with mixed results.

Unlike in other target cities, Chicago's mayor cordially welcomed Dr. King. Richard Daley had controlled Chicago for many years and had an unparalleled political machine. He was not ready to have his city disrupted by violence. He was ready to work with King to improve the economic and social conditions of his Black constituents. Daley made the resources of the city available to King and helped him at every turn. Ironically, Daley's help hindered Dr. King. It was almost impossible for King to find an issue that would ignite the Black community.

Although Chicago was ostensibly an integrated city, in fact its neighborhoods were segregated by race, a phenomenon known as *de facto segregation*. In an effort to jump-start his still undefined campaign, King now led a march from the Black area of the city into a White neighborhood. King's goal was to focus on the inequities of real estate practices by marching to Marquette Park and picketing a White real estate agency. At Marquette Park, George Lincoln Rockwell, the leader of the American Nazi Party, and men wearing the regalia of the Ku Klux Klan confronted King's group. Soon a rock-throwing melee broke out. King was bloodied when hit in the head by a rock. Police finally quelled the disturbance.

As television recorded the confrontation in Marquette Park, Chicago's racism was exposed to the nation. Americans listened as Martin Luther King, Jr., responding to a reporter's question, said that he had never seen hate in Mississippi like he had experienced in Chicago. In the days that followed, more marches into White neighborhoods were met with the same violent reaction.

Finally, the threat of a march into the neighboring community of Cicero brought the confrontation in Chicago to a head. At a meeting with King and his associates, Mayor Daley and the head of the Chicago

Board of Real Estate agreed to a plan for open housing in the city. The march on Cicero was cancelled and in King's view non-violence had prevailed. Unfortunately, as time passed, the promises for open housing were never fulfilled.

The events in Chicago were an excellent barometer of what happened to the civil rights movement when it moved North. As long as the movement attacked the traditional bastion of bigotry, the South, Northern Whites were willing to support it with words, actions, and money. When the movement came North, Whites were threatened. Their words now became epithets. Their actions turned to rock throwing. Their money stayed in their checkbooks. This response became known as White Backlash. Its slogan was *White Power.*[87]

Urban rioting was now replacing non-violent protest. Brooklyn, Philadelphia, and Atlanta were but a few of the cities buffeted by racial strife. There were major riots in Detroit and Newark in the summer of 1967. Forty-three people were killed in the seven-day uprising in Detroit. Twenty-three died in Newark. Across the nation there were pleas for law and order, and investigative committees were formed to identify the root causes of the disorders. The Commission on Civil Disorders in New Jersey, not surprisingly, attributed the basic causes of the riot to poor housing, poor education, and unemployment. It placed responsibility squarely on the shoulders of those in positions of authority. It stressed the importance for those in authority to treat all people with dignity and respect. It said that the time for promises and press releases was long past. It called on suburban America to recognize that its future is directly connected to what goes on in the cities.

Later, a National Advisory Commission on Civil Disorders headed by the former Governor of Illinois, Otto Kerner, said in its report of February 29, 1968, that "white racism was chiefly responsible for the explosive mixture of poverty, discrimination, and resentment in the black community." It concluded with the following statement: "What white Americans have never fully understood, but what the Negro can never forget, is that white society is deeply implicated in the ghetto.

The days of non-violent civil rights demonstrations seemed to end as riots took place in Harlem (1964); Watts (1965); Chicago and Cleveland (1966); Newark, Detroit, Tampa, Cincinnati, and Atlanta (1967); Washington, D.C. and Cleveland (1968). The cities listed represent only a small number of the disturbances recorded. During the summer of 1967, 164 disturbances of varying intensity took place in 128 cities. The above picture shows Ohio National Guardsmen called into the east district of Cleveland. July 24, 1968. *Image courtesy of Documentary Photo Aids.*

White institutions created it, white institutions maintain it, and white society condones it."[88] Thirty years later little has happened to alleviate the truth of that statement.

For Martin Luther King, Jr. 1967 was a frustrating year. He watched his efforts in Chicago dissipate. His leadership of the civil rights movement was being seriously challenged by Stokely Carmichael, the Black Panthers, Rap Brown, and others more oriented to direct action backed up by a gun, than to peaceful protest supported by prayer. Within the civil rights movement Dr. King's colleagues were increasingly disturbed with his new focus on politics. They knew that the civil rights movement needed the support of President Johnson. They also knew that Johnson, more than any of his predecessors had provided that support.

But now King was aligning himself with the anti-war movement and increasingly speaking out against the war in Vietnam. That April in New York, he lead a march of 125,000 people to the United Nations building to present a petition calling for an end of hostilities in Vietnam. He was challenging and embarrassing the President. His colleagues knew that the civil rights movement would be the loser in this struggle.

King was now floundering. His civil rights base was eroding. His anti-Vietnam crusade was rejected by the government and a large segment of society. His achievements were being perceived as passé, and the luster of his Nobel Peace Prize and many other awards was now tarnished. His most recent book, *Where Do We Go From Here? Chaos or Community* had received poor reviews. Then he was approached by a former Mississippi social worker, with Washington connections, Mrs. Marion Wright Edelman. Mrs. Edelman had been working on poverty programs. She told King of the many programs available for the poor that were unused because people were unaware of their existence. She also told him that members of Congress were sympathetic to the plight of the poor and would respond with more assistance if asked.[89]

King now had an issue tailored to his background and talents. It was an opportunity for him to realize his vision of expanding his role. It was an opportunity to do something fundamentally good. It was an opportunity to help the poor and destitute of all races: Black, White, Latin, and Asian. At the same time, it was an opportunity to reject those advocating violence and separation. He could once again seize the moral high ground. With the blessing of his colleagues in the Southern Christian Leadership Conference, he announced on December 4th that he was organizing a Poor Peoples' March on Washington. The march would take place the following spring. Its goal was an economic Bill of Rights that would include full employment and a guaranteed annual income. Its symbol would be a mule train and a wagon that would journey from Mississippi to Washington, D.C. and arrive on the day of the march.

National Guard reaction to a protest in Memphis, Tennessee on March 29,1968. Six days later Martin Luther King, Jr. was assassinated in Memphis. *Image courtesy of Documentary Photo Aids.*

❨

The history of a nation is more often the result of the unexpected than of the planned. In many cases it turns on momentous events. In 1968, American history was determined by a garbage men's strike. As Martin Luther King, Jr. and the members of SCLC commenced planning the Poor Peoples' March on Washington, the garbage men of Memphis, Tennessee, were embroiled in a wage dispute with Mayor Henry Loeb. On February 12th, the garbage men, most of whom were Black, went on strike. What began as a simple dispute over wages soon developed into a full-fledged racial battle between the predominantly Black union, Local 1733, and the White power structure of the City of Memphis.

The first week of April found Dr. King in Memphis supporting the garbage men's strike. The strike had lasted longer than anyone expected and had become increasingly violent. On April 3rd, King participated in a march through the center of the city. Black youths accompanying the marchers chanted: "Black power, black power." The marchers were met by police in riot gear. Soon pushing and shoving turned into nightsticks and tear gas. Then through the smoke shots were fired.

That evening Martin Luther King spoke to an overflowing audience at the Mason Temple Church. He spoke with conviction and said that the Negro race would some day reach "the Promised Land." However, prophetically, he said that he might not be with them on that day.[90] It was to be his last speech. The following day Martin Luther King, Jr. was standing on the balcony of the Lorraine Motel. On an adjacent rooftop James Earl Ray found King in the cross hairs of his telescopic sight. Ray took a deep breath and placed his finger on the trigger of the high powered rifle that was jammed into his shoulder. He exhaled slowly and increased the pressure of the trigger. A shot rang out. At approximately 6:30PM. Martin Luther King, Jr. was dead.

News of King's assassination momentarily stunned the nation. Then a firestorm swept the country. Riots and disturbances broke out in more than one hundred cities. The nation's capital was the scene of the worst riot. For the first time since the Civil War, armed U.S. soldiers were sent to protect the Capitol building. Fires raged out of control in the Northwest portion of the city. Looters ran up and down 14th Street just blocks from the White House. Elements of the 2nd Marine Division were flown from Camp Lejeune, North Carolina, to Washington. Nothing in their training had prepared these veterans of Vietnam for conducting an armed helicopter assault with the Washington Monument as their Landing Zone. As Army units augmented the Marines, martial law was imposed by the Military Police.

Martin Luther King, Jr. was buried in Atlanta, Georgia, on April 9, 1968. Three days earlier President Lyndon Johnson had declared a national day of mourning and ordered the American flag to be flown at half mast on all federal buildings. King's funeral was a mixture of celebrity and simplicity. Vice President Hubert Humphrey, Robert Kennedy, Richard Nixon, Harry Belafonte, New York Mayor John Lindsay, and Sidney Poitier were among the many celebrities present. But the simplicity of the proceedings reflected the man and his wishes. The night before he died, while speaking at the Mason Temple Church in Memphis, King had reflected on the possibility of his death. He told the audience that God had allowed him "to go to the mountain top" and see the Promised Land. He went on to say that he knew he might not be with them when they reached the Promised Land, but that he knew they would get there. He then told the audience that he wanted to be remembered not for his Nobel Prize, but for doing God's work. He wanted to be remembered not as a man who had received honors and mixed with the powerful of the world, but as a man who had dedicated his life to the service of his people. And so he was. There were no bands or columns of marching soldiers. King was brought to his funeral on a simple farm wagon drawn by two mules and followed by thousands of tear-streaked Black faces.

King's mission was over and America had yet to face its future. There were more questions than answers. Who would lead now that King was gone? Was the civil rights movement over? Did King's assassin act alone? Was there a conspiracy? Would Jim Crow return? For Black Americans the Promised Land now seemed but a distant hope.

NOTES

58. Rowan, p. 168

59. U.S. Army Forces Command, *Black Americans: A Military Perspective* (Fort McPherson, Georgia, January 1983) p. 11

60. Richard Kluger, *Simple Justice* (New York: Alfred A. Knopf, 1976), p.746

61. Low and Clift, p. 486

62. Wm. Roger Witherspoon, *Martin Luther King, Jr.: To The Mountaintop* (Garden City, New York: Doubleday and Company Inc.,1985), pp.32-33.

63. Jim Bishop, *The Days Of Martin Luther King, Jr.* (New York: G.P. Putnam & Sons, 1971), pp. 196-197

64. Bennett, p. 379

65. *Eyes on the Prize*, (Boston: Blackside Inc., 1986)

66. *Eyes on the Prize*, (Boston: Blackside Inc., 1986)

67. *The Search for Black Identity: Malcolm X*. Pleasantville, New York: Guidance Associates Sound Filmstrips, 1970

68. *Eyes on the Prize*, (Boston: Blackside Inc., 1986)

69. Bishop, p. 251

70. Bennett, p. 385

71. Bishop, p. 282

72. Bishop, p. 284

73. Bennett, p. 388

74. Bennett, p. 392

75. Stephen B. Oates, *Let The Trumpet Sound* (New York: Harper & Row Publishers, 1982) p. 232

76. *Eyes on the Prize*, (Boston: Blackside Inc., 1986)

77. Oates, p. 240

78. "Beckwith Trial Stirs Mississippi Ghosts," *Boston Sunday Globe* (January 16,1994) p. 1

79. Bishop, p. 232

80. Oates, pp. 256-257

81. "The Four Girls," *Boston Sunday Globe* (February 3, 1991), p. 15

82. Bishop, p. 390

83. Bennett, p. 417

84. Oates, p. 377

85. Bishop, p. 407

86. Boorstin and Kelley, p. 751

87. *Eyes on the Prize*, (Boston: Blackside Inc.,1986)

88. Bennett, p. 428

89. Bishop, p. 468

90. Oates, pp. 486-487

6

Closing the 20th Century

The Civil Rights Movement of the 1960s effectively died with the assassination of Dr. Martin Luther King, Jr. In the aftermath of this tragedy, Dr. Ralph Abernathy, King's longtime right-hand man and trusted confidant, assumed leadership of the Southern Christian Leadership Conference (SCLC). Dr. Abernathy had marched with King every step of the way and was well qualified to assume the mantle of leadership. He was intelligent, articulate, courageous, and honest, but he faced insurmountable odds in perpetuating Dr. King's legacy.

Ralph Abernathy assumed leadership of SCLC at the worst possible time. Prior to his death Martin Luther King was in the process of expanding his horizons and beginning his Poor People's Campaign. His actions had been controversial, and there was disagreement within SCLC as to the future course of the civil rights movement. Jesse Jackson was one of the more vocal opponents of the Poor People's Campaign. After King's assassination Jackson caused further strain within SCLC. He was quoted in the press as saying about King: "Yes, I was the last person he spoke to as I was cradling him in my arms." Jackson repeated the statement when he was interviewed on *The Today Show* the day after the assassination.[91] It wasn't true. Although some members of SCLC were furious with Jackson, Abernathy let the matter pass attributing Jackson's actions to the shock and confusion surrounding the assassination.[92] However, Jackson soon found himself in more serious trouble with the SCLC leadership.

Prior to his death Dr. King had placed Jackson in charge of a program called Operation Breadbasket. The purpose of the program was to target White owned companies doing business in the Black community and force them to hire Black employees, not just at the lower levels, but throughout the corporate hierarchy. The program had three levels of activity. First, the Black leadership would ask the targeted business to increase its number of Black employees. If this failed, the leadership would ask the Black community to boycott the business and its products. This action would then lead to negotiations and a settlement. The idea originated in Philadelphia, where the Reverend Leon Sullivan had been successfully increasing the number of jobs available to African Americans.[93]

Dr. King wanted the program to be implemented nationwide, but there were problems from the start. Jackson insisted on running the program from his headquarters in Chicago rather than in Atlanta, which was the headquarters of King and SCLC. The results were predictable. Operation Breadbasket became highly successful in the Chicago area, but it never truly grew into a national program.[94]

After King's death, Jackson proposed and Abernathy approved a new program called Black Expo. It was based on the idea that White businesses needed Black customers and Black Expo would provide an entrance for Blacks into the marketplace. Black Expo was basically a giant trade fair where White-owned businesses and some Black businesses displayed their wares. It attracted thousands of people by featuring entertainment from celebrities who donated their time and talent. In 1969 the SCLC received $66,000 as their share of the Black Expo proceeds. In 1970 the SCLC's share was reduced to $11,000.[95]

By 1971 the finances of the Black Expo were becoming controversial. Angela Parker, a young Black reporter for the *Chicago Tribune*, requested an interview with Ralph Abernathy. During the interview she showed Abernathy documents indicating that SCLC did not own Black Expo. It had been incorporated as a non-profit organization by a group of Chicago businessmen. Abernathy was stunned, and later he and other members of the SCLC leadership confronted Jackson. Following their discussions the SCLC leadership suspended Jackson for 60 days with pay while they further investigated the Black Expo matter. Jackson responded by immediately resigning from SCLC. He then organized Operation PUSH and embarked on the road that made him a national figure and presidential candidate.[96]

For all his favorable qualities, Abernathy lacked charisma, the one quality needed to lead the civil rights movement. He was not a man to inspire passion. He lacked the fire that makes others willing to forget personal agendas and come together in the face of danger for a cause. However, the death of the civil rights movement was not solely the result of Ralph Abernathy's leadership. In addition to confusion within the movement, there was the matter of the war in Vietnam. By 1968, the war was at its height in terms of combat and casualties. The nation's leaders were telling the public that victory was in sight, that there was "a light at the end of the tunnel." In February of that year the light went out as the Viet Cong unleashed their surprisingly successful Tet Offensive. As casualties mounted and the war dragged on with no apparent purpose, protests that had previously been confined to college campuses spread across the nation. The national consciousness focused on the issue of Vietnam with a passion. Division and disagreement crossed racial, economic, religious, and social lines. Families were split with one son fighting in Vietnam while another refused service and fled to Canada. The nation had moved on to more immediate concerns and there was nothing Ralph Abernathy or any other Black leader could do to refocus attention on the plight of the Black community.

The high percentage of Black Americans assigned to combat units and the disparity between Black and White casualty rates in Vietnam were legitimate concerns that never quite received the attention they deserved. The disastrous effect of Project 100,000 ensured an ever-increasing casualty rate among Blacks and was an embarrassment to both the Defense Department and the Administration. So, too, was the draft even though a lottery system had by then been initiated. As the war drew to a close in the mid-1970s, the Nixon administration implemented the concept of the All-Volunteer Force. An All-Volunteer Force eliminated two political problems:

- The military obligation opposed by affluent whites was no longer a problem.
- The sticky problem of the racial composition of the Armed Forces was no longer an issue.

The politicians now had a comfortable explanation for most constituent queries and complaints—"The Armed Forces are volunteers."

☾

The All-Volunteer Force and newly implemented Affirmative Action programs did have a positive impact on Black America. After the Armed Forces were integrated in the early 1950s, the military was one place a Black American could expect an equal opportunity. Now in the 1970s, the opportunities were even greater. To their credit the Armed Forces implemented Affirmative Action in the spirit that was originally proposed by President Johnson, searching for qualified persons to be advanced on the basis of their abilities. In particular, Black officers were rising through the ranks and were now being selected as General and Flag Officers. The glass ceiling had been broken. In 1991, as the United States joined in a major conflict in the Middle East, the first major combat deployment since the Vietnam War, a Black soldier, General Colin L. Powell, led its forces.

As Black America entered the decade of the 1970s, it could look back at the achievements of the past quarter century with a sense of pride and accomplishment. Jim Crow laws had been eradicated even though approximately 17 states still maintained anti-miscegenation statutes. In Virginia, a Black man and a White woman had been convicted of miscegenation and were released from prison only after they agreed not to reside in Virginia for a period of 25 years. In 1967, the U.S Supreme Court overturned their conviction, *Loving v. Virginia*, and declared miscegenation laws unconstitutional.[97] By 1990, interracial marriages in the United States had more than quadrupled, but the total number of these marriages remained small. In 1992, less than 1% of all marriages united Blacks with people of another race.[98]

Individual Black Americans were finally receiving recognition for their achievements. Sidney Poitier had been awarded an Oscar. Robert Weaver became the first Black member of the Cabinet when President Lyndon Johnson appointed him as Secretary of Housing and Urban Development in 1966. Jackie Robinson had integrated baseball and now professional Black athletes, like football's Jim Brown, were widely admired. By 1996, Black athletes were the dominant figures in most professional sports, particularly in basketball and football. In that year the newly constructed Center Court at the National Tennis Center in New York City was named after the late Arthur Ashe, a Black tennis player who had learned his sport on the segregated courts of Richmond, Virginia.

African Americans had made significant gains in the political arena as well. In 1966, Edward Brooke of Massachusetts became the first African American elected to the U. S. Senate since the days of Reconstruction.[99] Shirley Chisholm followed in Brooke's footsteps when in 1968, she became the first African American woman elected to the U. S. House of Representatives.[100] By 1972, there were 2,264 Black elected officials in state legislatures and local governments across the country.[101] And in 1973, the cities of Detroit and Los Angeles had Black mayors, Coleman Young and Tom Bradley.[102] Most importantly, Thurgood Marshall became the first Black Supreme Court Justice.

Black achievements were not limited to individuals. The efforts of the Civil Rights Movement and of President Johnson's Great Society had reduced the number of Blacks at the lowest end of the wage scale and increased the percentage at the upper end. By 1967, for the first time, more than half of all Black workers held white collar, craftsman, or operative jobs. Employment in these occupations was 70% larger in 1970 than in 1960.[103]

Enrollment of Black students in the nation's colleges rose. In 1964, approximately 250,000 African Americans were enrolled in college. By 1976, that figure had increased to 817,000. In 1977, more than one million African Americans were enrolled in college. Two factors encouraged this dramatic increase in college enrollments. First, as a direct result of the Civil Rights Movement, the nation's traditionally non-Black colleges adopted open enrollment policies. Second was the increase in the number of community colleges.[104]

Significant changes in campus attitudes and activities accompanied the increased enrollment of Black students at predominantly White colleges. A prime example of change took place at the University of Vermont. Since 1893, the featured event at Winter Carnival on this picturesque campus in America's Whitest State was the *Kake Walk*. Kake Walk itself consisted "of two nights of elaborately choreographed skits performed by White students dressed as minstrels complete with Blackface and kinky-haired wigs." The highlight of the evening was the competition of *walkin' fo de kake*. The competition featured two-man teams of fraternity brothers in blackface performing a high stepping dance simulating "something originally done by slaves performing for their masters' favor."[105] As the number of Black students on campus increased, Kake Walk became increasingly controversial. Students and faculty aggressively protested against it. Finally, in 1969, the university terminated the objectionable practice. However, at the beginning of the twenty-first century, the subject of Kake Walk remains a divisive issue among the alumni.

❆

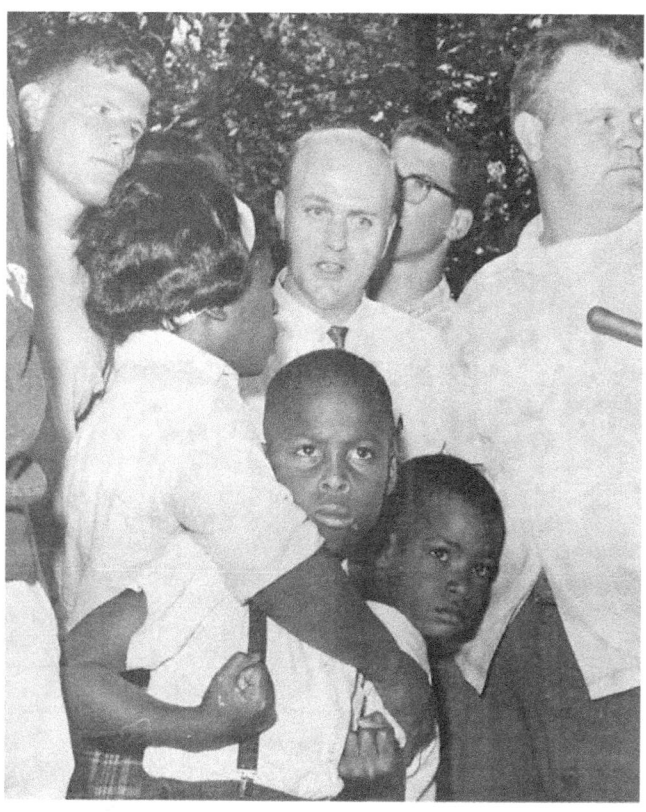

School integration was also resisted in the North. The above picture, taken in 1964, shows a mother attempting to enroll her son in a predominantly White elementary school in Malverne, L.I., N.Y. *Image courtesy of Documentary Photo Aids.*

The face of the nation's elementary and secondary schools also changed. The 1954 Supreme Court ruling in *Brown v. The Board of Education* had addressed the problem of *de jure* segregation, a problem primarily associated with schools in the Southern states. Integration of public education was now mandatory, but it would be anything but peaceful. The South's resistance to the Brown ruling was intense and violent. This reaction was expected. What was unexpected was the reaction to school integration in the North.

Protesters being arrested in Greenville, N.C. in 1969. They were attempting to march through the city on their way to the state capitol at Raleigh to protest school segregation. *Image courtesy of Documentary Photo Aids.*

The Supreme Court's decision in the Brown case was silent with respect to *de facto* segregation of schools in other parts of the country, particularly those in the North. Unlike the South, where Blacks and Whites generally lived close to one another, in the North, Blacks and Whites lived in a pattern of separate enclaves. The result of these living patterns was segregation in fact or *de facto* segregation. In 1971, the Supreme Court began to address this problem when it ruled, in the case of *Swann v. Charlotte-Mecklenburg*, in favor of busing students to achieve the integration of schools.[106]

A year after the Swann decision, segregation in Boston's school system was challenged when the case of *Morgan v. Hennigan* was filed in the U. S. District Court in Massachusetts. On June 21, 1974, Judge W. Arthur Garrity ruled that the Boston School Committee had acted with intent to segregate its schools. With only three months remaining before the opening day of school, Judge Garrity was hard pressed to implement a plan for desegregation. His initial plan called for busing students from Roxbury to South Boston. Roxbury was a predominantly Black community. South Boston, or Southie as it is affectionately known, was a White neighborhood distinguished for its strong opposition to integration.

Predictably, this first effort was a dismal failure. When Black students arrived at South Boston High School, a stone-throwing crowd met them. As the school year progressed White families boycotted the schools and had their children privately tutored. On one occasion, a local Black leader was warned to keep the Black students from attending school the next day. It was later learned that a crowd had planned to overturn and burn the black students' buses. On normal school days there would be ten to fifteen fights, and tension, rather than learning, was the atmosphere of the classroom.[107]

The following year, Judge Garrity expanded the busing program with the number of students to be bused increasing to 25,000. His objective was to obtain a more balanced racial mix in all of Boston's schools. Among the communities now affected was the poor working-class, pre-dominantly White neighborhood adjacent to the old Boston Navy Yard, Charlestown. The parents of Charlestown rebelled at the prospect of Black students attending Charlestown High and their children being sent to the predominantly Black high school in Roxbury. Like parents in other communities, Charlestonians who could afford it sent their children to private or parochial schools.

When school opened, Charlestown students refused to attend. Their parents conducted protests. When the White students returned to school, the tensions that had poisoned the academic environment in South Boston the previous year were repeated in Charlestown. White students taunted and physically attacked the Black students. Finally, a group of Black students presented the principal with a petition that de-manded, among other grievances, that Whites stop calling Blacks *nig-gers*. Whites in turn presented their own petition. It accused Black boys of making obscene gestures at White girls. As tensions increased, the headmaster, Mr. Frank Powell, suffered from hypertension and had to be granted a leave of absence. It was only October. In January, the White students staged a sit-in on the school's main staircase. The Black students barely made it safely out of the school that day. Somehow they completed the school year, despite the dangerous conditions and hostile atmosphere.[108]

The South Boston and Charlestown experiences are extreme examples, but by no means isolated incidents, of White reaction to school busing. Black reaction to the busing program was significantly different. It is important to note that Black parents also had reservations about the wisdom of the busing program. What is conspicuous is the absence of violent behavior among Black parents when White students arrived at previously all-Black schools. Similarly, Black students did not greet their White counterparts with violence. Admittedly, there were tensions at Black schools and some White students were taunted and harassed, but these incidents paled in comparison to the actions of Whites in general.

Even though Court-ordered busing ended in Boston in 1987, thousands of students were still bused to schools outside their neighborhoods in 1999. In the 25 years since Judge Garrity ordered desegregation, the demographics of Boston have changed. In 1975 the Boston schools were 49% White, 39% Black, 9% Hispanic, and 3% Asian while in 1999 those figures were 15% White, 49% Black, 26% Hispanic, and 9% Asian.[109] Although these figures reflect past White flight to the suburbs, the Boston of today is a more diverse community. It continues to be under a court order to maintain a desegregated school system. At the close of the century however, the mayor was proposing to build five new neighborhood schools and to eliminate future busing. Although the plan would have to be approved by a federal court, that alone doesn't explain the tepid opposition to the Mayor's proposal.[110]

According to CNN Boston Bureau Chief Bill Delaney, "Many Bostonians we spoke with—White, Black, Hispanic, and Asian—agreed that if busing failed to integrate as some people once hoped, its even greater failure lay in shifting the spotlight off the quality of schools and onto the more mechanical issue of sitting White and Black children next to each other." Parents with school age children are now more concerned with the quality of education. They are concerned that the Boston schools are not preparing their children to compete with their suburban counterparts for the high tech jobs offered in the marketplace.[111] As stated by Leonard Atkins of the Boston chapter of the NAACP: "The Boston education system is worse than it was twenty-five years ago. They are giving a bad education to all students."[112]

❨

The assassinations of Martin Luther King, Jr. and Senator Robert F. Kennedy were followed by the election of Richard Nixon as president. With the ascendance of a Republican administration, America now marched in a new direction. Traditional Republican values returned to dominate the political landscape: eliminate government programs, reduce welfare, encourage business, be tough on crime, etc. These philosophies were blended with an altruistic return to a spirit of individualism, the belief that each man, not the government, was responsible for his personal situation. In this atmosphere White America re-evaluated its responsibilities to its Black brethren and concluded that it had done enough.[113]

As the policies of the Nixon administration increasingly reflected the national mood, it wasn't surprising that, compared to Whites, the median income of Black families began to drop and unemployment rates began to rise. In 1970 the mean income ratio between Blacks and Whites was 61%. By 1973 it dropped to 58%. Conversely, in 1975, the unemployment rate for Blacks was 13.7% as opposed to 7.6% for Whites.[114] What was surprising, however, was the Nixon Administration's support for Affirmative Action programs.

The term "Affirmative Action" was first used in President Kennedy's 1961 executive order creating a Committee on Equal Employment Opportunity. It is generally understood to mean affording every person an equal opportunity in matters of education and economics. It has been described by Owen Fiss, a professor at the Yale School of Law, as "a means of eradicating the caste structure that now mars our society and has its roots in slavery and the segregation of Jim Crow."[115] The concept was most eloquently articulated by President Johnson in his analogy of the track race between a world-class runner and a formerly shackled prisoner. During his 1965 speech at Howard University, Johnson emphasized that, although both runners were to run the same distance over the same track, the competition clearly wasn't equal.

Johnson demonstrated his commitment to Affirmative Action by issuing Executive Order 11246. This order required federal contractors to take affirmative action to ensure equality of employment opportunity without regard to race, religion, and national origin.[116] However, the plan to implement the order, by establishing goals and timetables, was unable to overcome resistance from unions and contractors. The Nixon Administration's 1969 order expanding the Johnson goals and timetables was rooted in President Nixon's belief that "A good job is as basic and important civil right as a basic education." This order, known as "The Philadelphia Order" because it specifically targeted the construction trades in Philadelphia, was significant. It did not establish quotas, but it did require federal contractors to show affirmative action in meeting the goals of increased minority employment.[117]

The principles of Affirmative Action were equally important in the field of education. Despite court rulings in the 1950s, the percentage of Black students attending college in 1965 remained at 4.9%.[118] By the late 1960s and early 1970s, Affirmative Action measures assisted in increasing the number of Black students in college. As in the case of the construction trades, there was resistance to Affirmative Action in education.

In California, Allan Bakke sued to be admitted to the University of California at Davis medical school. Bakke contended that the University's policy of reserving 16 places for minority students, from the 100 slots allocated for its entering class, was discriminatory. The U.S. Supreme Court heard the case. The Court issued its ruling on June 28, 1978 in a 5-4 split decision. Justice Lewis Powell wrote for the majority that "while Davis' program was unconstitutional, colleges and universities could still use race as one of several factors in their attempts to create a diverse student body." The heart of Powell's argument was that diversity in higher education represented a "compelling state interest," and for that reason affirmative action programs that did not use quotas could be regarded as constitutional.[119]

The Bakke case was to higher education what the 1954 Brown case was to secondary education. Bakke provided the foundation for Affirmative Action programs for the next 20 years and was consistently the subject of heated debate. In the 1990s, Justice Powell's basic premise was challenged in California. This time the California Legislature provided the forum for change. It passed a constitutional amendment, commonly known as Proposition 209, prohibiting Affirmative Action. Ratified by the electorate on November 5, 1996, the amendment stated: "The state shall not discriminate against, or grant preferential treatment to any individual or group on the basis of race, sex, color, ethnicity, or national origin in the operation of public employment, public education, or public contracting".[120]

On November 11,1996, a coalition of civil rights groups, including the NAACP, filed a complaint against Proposition 209 in the U.S. District Court for the Northern District of California. On November 27,1996, Judge Thelton Henderson issued a preliminary injunction preventing its implementation. On April 8, 1997, the Ninth District Court of Appeals Panel overturned Judge Henderson's injunction. The U.S. Supreme Court denied an appeal on September 4, 1997, and the amendment was added to the California Constitution.[121] The chilling affect of the amendment became an immediate reality. That year the University of California Berkley School of Law admitted only one Black first-year student. The previous year 20 African Americans had entered as first-year students.[122]

Universities in Texas opened the 1997 fall semester, under a court order to dismantle Affirmative Action policies. The order was the result of a discrimination case initiated by a White student who had been denied admission to law school. In its ruling the court said that race could not be used as a factor in admissions. In turn, the Texas Attorney General interpreted the court's ruling to apply to financial aid, recruiting, and undergraduate programs. The immediate result was that out of the 6,500 members of the freshman class at the University of Texas only 150 were African Americans. That represented one-half the number admitted the previous year.[123]

California and Texas provided clear evidence that elimination of Affirmative Action programs would deprive Black Americans an equal opportunity for higher education. Nevertheless, the movement to eliminate these programs rippled across America. Governor Jeb Bush of Florida proposed replacing Affirmative Action programs with his *Talented 20* rule. *Talented 20* guarantees college admission to all high school seniors who graduate in the top 20% of their class. Unfortunately, Governor Bush's staff predicted that, under *Talented 20*, approximately 40% fewer minority students would be eligible for college admission than under the existing Affirmative Action program.[124] It's ironic that as California, Texas, and Florida dismantled Affirmative Action, the prestigious women's college in Massachusetts, Smith College, was installing its first Black president, Ruth J. Simmons.

White America fears Affirmative Action. It represents loss of opportunity. It is viewed as an impediment to future financial success and the good life. Opposition to Affirmative Action is most often expressed in the question: "Why should I be punished for my ancestors actions? Slavery ended 135 years ago, after the Civil War."

Such reasoning fails to acknowledge that 135 years is a historical minute. It forgets that White Americans have consistently benefited from the racist practices of the past. It fails to recognize the obstacles placed in the path of Black Americans attempting to climb the ladder of success. It overlooks the wisdom of Owen Fiss' observation that America still suffers from a caste structure spawned by slavery and raised by Jim Crow. It perpetuates misunderstandings that widen, rather than bridge, the gulf separating Whites and Blacks.

❨

The Nixon administration's support of Affirmative Action provided a slight glimmer of hope in a bleak political landscape. The glimmer was extinguished on June 17, 1972, when Frank Wills, a Black security guard, reported a break-in at the Democratic National Committee Headquarters in a Washington, D.C., hotel complex known as Watergate. Unwittingly, Wills set in motion a series of events exposing a national political scandal that ended with Richard Nixon becoming the first president to resign from office. Once again the nation focused on a single divisive issue, *Watergate,* and the needs of the Black America were forced to take a back seat.

While the nation focused on the political turmoil of the Vietnam and Watergate years, economic and social conditions in the inner cities worsened. In 1982, Ken Auletta, a writer for the *New Yorker* magazine, coined a new term to describe people living in the inner cities whom "he broadly classified as individuals with behavioral and income deficiencies." [125] He called them the *Underclass.* In 1992 Dimitri Papadimitriou, in a paper entitled *Employment Policy, Community Development, and the Underclass,* expanded the definition of underclass as follows:

> I consider as members of the underclass, individuals residing in urban centers, mostly in inner city areas. Their neighborhoods experience concentrated poverty and joblessness, and violence, and lack of community supporting institutions. Those individuals who are employed are working poor and their education is at the high-school level or below; and a good number of them are single parents, either male or female heads of households. Finally, I include as members of the underclass, a significant fraction of the more 45% of children under 6 years of age and individuals under the age of 18 who live below the poverty line. Even though only a fraction of those living in poverty reside in these neighborhoods—about 21 percent of all persons and 34 percent of blacks that live in the inner city areas were below the poverty line in 1994—escaping from there requires confronting and dealing with a plethora of insurmountable obstacles. It should be noted that members of the underclass are not likely to include Jews, Irish, or Italians, nor are they only African Americans. If it were only a Black problem, it would disregard the two-thirds of African Americans who are not poor, and the two

thirds of the poor residing in the inner city who are not Black. African Americans are over represented in the underclass.[126]

Among African Americans the underclass is dominated by young males who are undereducated and unemployed. Many come from broken families. Their high school dropout rate is 18% Their unemployment rate approximates 40%. The leading cause of death among this group is homicide, and a disproportionate number are in prison. They live in a world of necessary machismo, one that considers fathering children out of wedlock and committing crimes as rites of passage.[127] It is a philosophy that has grown out of the hopelessness of their environment, and it perpetuates a cycle of despair that passes from one generation to another.

Breaking the cycle of despair has proved to be almost impossible. The few jobs available are minimum-wage positions. For most young fathers the better option is to not marry as the mother and child will be financially better off on welfare. Then, too, there is the appeal of the drug trade where quick money can be made and past criminal records are assets, not prohibitions to employment. However, a life of crime is not conducive to establishing a family and roots in the community. For these and many other reasons, not the least of which has been indifference by the federal government, the plight of the underclass has remained unresolved.

The 1980s also witnessed the emergence of a middle class of affluent African Americans. This new class of African Americans was largely the product of the opportunities created by the sacrifices of the civil rights marchers of the 1960s and the affirmative action laws of the 1970s. The needs of the middle class were not so apparent yet they were equally pressing.

The middle-class African American was able to acquire financial stability and the material things expected of a middle-class lifestyle. What was missing was unqualified acceptance by the rest of society, both White and Black. Whites looked at the Black middle class as either a threat or as the product of favoritism spawned by Affirmative Action.

Whites also expected the middle-class Black to return to the ghetto and solve the problems of unemployment, crime, drugs, illiteracy, and illegitimacy that local, state, and federal governments had been unable to solve. Underclass Blacks viewed the Black middle class with envy and resentment. Even some of the middle class fell prey to old stereotypes of White superiority.

Kenneth Glover of Manhattan, New York, is a Black financial director for Drexel Burnham Lambert, Inc. In a 1989 *Time* magazine article, *Between Two Worlds*, Glover talked of a situation where he telephoned a prospective client, a Black executive. The executive agreed to meet with Glover to discuss an investment. Their meeting lasted only ten minutes. Later, the executive called to have his account transferred to a White investment advisor. Glover believed the Black executive succumbed to the stereotypical perception that a White account executive would better manage his money. Glover feelings were aptly expressed when he said: "The White man's ice is colder."[128]

By the late 1990s, the Black middle class was enjoying unprecedented prosperity. Surveys consistently revealed that Blacks considered themselves better off financially than ever before and that they expected their job opportunities and their family incomes to rise in the next ten years. The booming economy accounts for some of this success. However, much of the success is the result of a resurgence in self-confidence and self-determination among the Black middle class.[129] Nevertheless, old problems persist. Black executives find that, no matter how well they are doing, they are still economically behind their White counterparts. Black unemployment remains at more than twice that of Whites. Black median income in 1997 reached $34,644, yet that was still $21,278 less than the average for Whites.[130]

❨

In 1982, the Reverend Jesse Jackson announced his candidacy for the office of President of the United States. Jackson's candidacy was greeted with mixed reaction: a combination of hope, seriousness, or ridicule—

depending on the color, personal agenda, or political persuasion of the critic. In 1986, Jackson again ran for the presidency. This time his success in the national primaries silenced his critics. It also proved that a Black candidate with a clearly articulated platform could win the support of large blocks of White voters. One more barrier had been broken, and by the 1990s, both major political parties were actively looking to Colin Powell in their quest to occupy the White House. Although he declared himself a Republican, Powell declined to run for the nation's highest office.

Jesse Jackson's candidacies for the presidency were highly visible and newsworthy events primarily because of the office he was seeking. By then the electorate had long accepted Black politicians. The cities of Los Angeles, New York, Chicago, Atlanta, and Washington, D.C., had Black mayors. Across the country Blacks were holding offices as sheriffs, selectmen, town clerks, and justices of the peace. In the U. S. Congress the Black caucus was a potent political bloc, and in 1992, Carol Mosley Braun became the first African American woman elected to the United States Senate.

Opportunity seemed endless in the 1980s, as African Americans came to prominence in a variety of fields. Debbie Thomas won the U.S. and World figure skating titles, followed by a Bronze medal in the Winter Olympics. Alice Walker won the Pulitzer Prize for her riveting novel *The Color Purple*. Oprah Winfrey began her sensational career as a talk show host. Barbara Harris became the world's first woman Anglican Bishop. Bill Cosby's humor captured the hearts of all Americans, particularly the young. From 1983-1985, Dr. Mae Jemison served as an Area Peace Corps Medical Officer for Sierra Leone and Liberia in West Africa. In 1987, she joined the National Aeronautics and Space Administration; and in 1993, as a member of the crew of space shuttle Endeavor, she became the first woman of color to go into space.

On October 23, 1989, Charles Stuart reported to the Boston police that, while he and his wife were driving home from birthing class, a Black man jumped into their car. He claimed the man shot and killed his wife Carol. Stuart himself was seriously wounded. The police immediately initiated a search of the Black neighborhood known as Mission Hill. They soon had a suspect, a thirty-nine-year-old drifter with a long criminal record, William Bennett. After raiding the homes of Bennett's friends and relatives, the police arrested him on November 11, 1989. The sensational story of a Black man killing a pregnant White woman and her unborn child was a bonanza for the media. Soon Bennett was all but convicted in the public's mind. The case then took a dramatic turn as evidence began to shift the focus of the investigation onto the husband. As the pressure mounted, Charles Stuart committed suicide, jumping from the Tobin Bridge that spans the Charles River. William Bennett was released from custody.

The Stuart case tragically highlights the gulf between Black and White America today. Stuart's claim that a Black man killed his wife was assumed to be true. The police never considered Stuart a suspect until later. Meanwhile, the Mission Hill community had been dramatically disrupted. The media frenzy had focused on Black crime. The civil rights of William Bennett, his friends, and his relatives had been trampled. The achievements of African Americans in the 1980s—economic, political, entertainment, religious, and athletic meant nothing. The White community assumed William Bennett's guilt. He was Black. He must have done it.

Ten years later the sores of the Stuart case continued to fester in Boston. In an October 20, 1999, issue of the *Boston Globe*, former police commissioner Francis Roach blamed the inept investigation and arrest of Bennett on the District Attorney's office. The former district attorney, Newman Flanagan, accused Roach of rewriting history to win re-election to the Boston City Council. Mission Hill residents remember the death of Carol Stuart and her unborn child with sadness and the actions of the police with resentment and distrust. Boston's reputation as the cradle of liberty remains under a cloud of racial injustice.

❬

As the decade of the 1980s drew to a close so too did the illustrious career of Thurgood Marshall. From his earliest days in the legal office of the NAACP to his role as a Supreme Court Justice, Marshall had always been at the center of controversy. True to form his retirement sparked a political firestorm when President George Bush nominated Clarence Thomas to fill Marshall's seat. Thomas' legal qualifications for the job were impeccable. The problem stemmed from his conservative views on politically sensitive issues such as Affirmative Action and abortion. His strict interpretation of the Constitution was, in itself, enough to ensure heated confirmation hearings. Then on the eve of his Senate confirmation, a former assistant at the Department of Justice accused Thomas of sexual harassment. His accuser was a little known professor from Texas, Anita Hill. The decade of the 1990s opened with the spectacle of a public hearing on the sexual relationship between a Black woman and a Black man, each of whom were highly respected in their chosen professions. When it ended, Clarence Thomas assumed his seat on the Supreme Court, Anita Hill returned to Texas, and Thurgood Marshall continued his retirement.

The 1990s also began with the poignant return of four middle-aged men to a department store in Greensboro, North Carolina. On February 1, 1990, Joseph McNeil, Jibreel Khazan (formerly known as Ezell Blair Jr.), Franklin McCain, and David Richmond sat down at the lunch counter in the Woolworth's store. The Black manager and popping flashbulbs greeted them. Thirty years earlier they had been evicted for sitting at the same counter, and their act of defiance had helped spark the movement to end segregation. A picture of the four men, picked up by the Associated Press and flashed across the country, brought back memories of a time when people of all races and creeds united and fought against the evil of segregation and racism.

By 1994, the euphoria of that unity was a thing of the past. Now the new leader of the Nation of Islam, Louis Farrakhan, was attacking Whites and particularly Jews. Farrakhan blamed Jewish merchants, bankers and investors for most of the economic problems facing Black

America and in one of his less temperate remarks compared the Jews to bloodsuckers.[131] Although he inflamed passions and resentments, Farrakhan could not be dismissed by the White or Black establishments. Much of what he said was true. He preached the concept of self-sufficiency previously espoused by Malcolm X. He was opposed to alcohol and drug abuse, teen pregnancy, the breakdown of the family, and lack of education. As proof that his positions were valid, he could point with considerable pride to the behavior and accomplishments of his followers.[132]

On October 16,1995, Farrakhan led a Million Man March in Washington, D.C., He called it a National Day of Atonement. The goal was to dispel the myth of all Black males being convicts, hustlers, and pimps and replace it with one of self-confident culturally aware men.[133] The spectacle of one million black men marching, without incident, and professing a commitment to their family responsibilities was indeed impressive. Two years later Black women conducted a similar march in Philadelphia.

☾

If the Stuart case was viewed as an aberration by some, two events in California made clear to any thoughtful observer the severe divide in America's race relations. On a summer night in Los Angeles in 1991, Rodney King, a Black man, got behind the wheel of his car drunk. Soon he was the center of a high-speed chase with the police. When the chase ended, King was taken from his car and beaten within an inch of his life by a group of White police officers. Their actions that night were watched approvingly by their sergeant supervisor. Not so approvingly, their actions were recorded on a video camera by a nearby witness. King was arrested and charged with drunken driving, resisting arrest, and a myriad of other offenses. However, it was the police themselves who eventually sat in the dock.

When the tape of King's brutal beating became public knowledge, the police officers involved were tried for abusing King's civil rights. The trial was sensational news and dominated the press, television, and talk shows for weeks. Finally, an all White jury acquitted the police officers. Immediately, the long festering frustrations of the Black community toward the Los Angeles police exploded in a riot. It was reminiscent of Watts in 1965. At the height of the riot, an unsuspecting truck driver named Reginald Denny was pulled from his truck and beaten by a group of Black youths. Denny's offense was that he was White. He was attacked as misguided recompense for the beating the police had administered to King. Ironically, before the disturbance could be quelled, Los Angeles authorities turned to Rodney King for help. King went on television asking the rioters to stop. In a poignant moment, he wondered aloud why it wasn't possible for the races to live together in peace. When the riot was over Reginald Denny's attackers were arrested, tried, and convicted. The police officers that had attacked Rodney King were re-tried in Federal Court on violations of the civil rights laws and convicted. The city of Los Angeles returned to being a place of unending sunshine and uneasy peace.

On another summer night in Los Angeles, this time in 1994, Nicole Brown Simpson and her friend Ron Goldman were found outside Nicole's apartment with their throats cut. Within days Nicole's famous husband, Hall of Fame football player O. J. Simpson, was charged with the murders. Once again there was a sensational trial. For more than a year, the electronic and print media saturated the public with stories and theories ranging from the responsible to the ridiculous. However, when it was finally over an all-Black jury found O. J. Simpson innocent. There was no riot this time, but the country was clearly split along racial lines with cheers coming from the Black community and anger from the White. In a subsequent civil action an all-White jury found Simpson guilty of wrongful death. Once again, the country was split along racial lines.

❝

The trials of O.J. Simpson and Rodney King exposed a problem that has been long known to the Black community and widely denied by the White community—institutional racism in law enforcement. As the impact of skin color on law enforcement became increasingly clear, America began to awaken to another form of racism, racial profiling. The practice was not something new. The Kerner Commission on Civil Disorder had identified it as early as 1967. However, with the advent of the war on drugs in the 1980s, racial profiling became a legitimate police practice.[134]

As Americans became increasingly concerned about substance abuse, politicians of every persuasion demanded the government take action. Predictably federal, state and local governments attacked the problem with law enforcement programs. These programs were designed to crack down on drug dealing in the streets. In New York there was Operation Pressure Point. In Memphis there was Operation Invincible. Chicago and Los Angeles had Operations Clean Sweep and Hammer. The targets of these programs were poor urban neighborhoods where drug dealing was easy to detect.

The success of the above programs, evidenced by an increased number of arrests and convictions of Black Americans for drug offenses, fueled the perception that most drug dealers and users were Black. In fact, according government reports, 80% of the country's cocaine users were White.[135] Nevertheless, the perception prevailed. Soon law enforcement agencies were using a drug courier profile to train their officers. That profile had unmistakable racial overtones. For example, in 1985, the Florida Department of Highway Safety and Motor Vehicles issued a document called "The Common Characteristics of Drug Couriers." Among other points, it instructed troopers "to be cautious of drivers wearing lots of gold, or who do not fit the vehicle and of ethnic groups associated with the drug trade." [136]

Armed with the drug courier profile law officers, searching for illegal drugs, began indiscriminately stopping Black drivers on the nation's highways. In what is called a *pretext stop*, police will stop a vehicle on the pretext that the driver has committed a traffic violation or that the vehicle has faulty equipment. Once stopped, the driver will then be questioned about drugs and the vehicle will be searched. Victims of the pretext stop argued that it violated the probable cause requirement of the 4th Amendment of the U.S. Constitution. However, in the case of *Whren v. U.S*, the Supreme Court ruled in 1996 "that any traffic offense committed by a driver was a legitimate legal basis for a stop, regardless of the officer's subjective state of mind."[137] The Court's decision opened the door for all Black Americans to experience the abuse of racial profiling.

❨

Americans love to drive. Their automobiles are both a necessity and a means of entertainment. But, for Black Americans the Whren decision has taken the joy from driving and replaced it with a fear of "driving while black" (DWB). In 1996 police apprehended George Washington and Daryl Hicks as they drove into the parking garage of a Santa Monica hotel. They were handcuffed, interrogated, and finally released. The arresting officers explained their actions on the grounds that one of the men looked nervous.[138]

In 1997 Aaron Campbell was pulled over by Orange County deputy sheriffs on the Florida Turnpike. His offense was an illegal lane change. Campbell identified himself as a major in the Metro-Dade Police Department. The stop resulted in Campbell being wrestled to the ground, pepper sprayed, and arrested. Campbell later said that he "went from an ordinary citizen and decorated police officer to a criminal in a matter of minutes."[139]

In Portland, Maine, Michael Stoval, a 35-year-old lawyer, passed a police car going in the opposite direction. The officer made a U-turn and followed Stoval for several blocks. Also in Portland, Judith Hyman was driving with her son who is Black and his girlfriend who is White. Hyman was stopped for no apparent reason. The officer said he wanted to ensure she was wearing her seat belt.[140]

In 1997, Charles and Etta Carter, an elderly couple from Pennsylvania, were driving in Maryland. It was their 40th wedding anniversary. The state police stopped them. Their car was searched by drug-sniffing dogs. During the search their belongings, including their daughter's wedding dress, were strewn along the highway. Although the search took considerable time, Mrs. Carter wasn't allowed to use the restroom. The officers were afraid she would run away. No drugs were found and no ticket was issued.[141]

The experiences of Charles and Etta Carter, Michael Stoval, Judith Hyman, and the others aptly describe the problem of driving while Black. DWB hasn't simply taken the joy out of driving. It has also undermined public confidence in law enforcement agencies and widened the gap between Black and White Americans. The Black experience in America continues to be radically different from that of White America.

❬

After the death of the University of Maryland's Black basketball star, Len Bias, America's war on drugs in the 1980s focused on the sale and use of cocaine in its two forms, crack and powder. Powdered cocaine is usually snorted through the nose and produces a slow, less intense high. Crack cocaine is smoked and gives a fast, intense high. Experts considered crack to be the more addictive form of cocaine for two reasons: the short high encouraged repeated use and it was affordable.[142] Although Bias died of an overdose of powdered cocaine, the media attention surrounding his death focused on the use of crack. Crack quickly became a plague of the inner city. It was viewed as the primary cause of violence and crime. In 1986 and 1988, Congress passed laws making penalties for the use of crack more severe than for the use of powdered cocaine. Possession of .5 grams of crack now required a mandatory five-year sentence.

The combination of police operations focusing on the inner cities and mandatory sentencing for the use of crack has imprisoned a disproportionate number of African Americans. Although approximately two-thirds of crack users are White or Hispanic, defendants convicted of crack possession in 1994 were 84.5% Black, 10.3% White, and 5% Hispanic. Offenders convicted of dealing crack were 88.3% Black, 4.1% White, and 7.1% Hispanic. On the other hand, the statistics for the less severe penalties relating to offenses for the use and sale of powdered cocaine are revealing. Defendants for simple possession of powdered cocaine were 58% White, 26.7% Black, and 15% Hispanic. Convictions for powdered cocaine dealers were 32% White, 27.4% Black, and 39.3% Hispanic. In 1997, representatives of President Clinton's administration publicly admitted that the effect of crack cocaine on the human body is little different from that of powdered cocaine and that sentencing guidelines should be the same for both. Nevertheless, because of the existing disparity in sentencing laws and the focus of the "war on drugs" on the inner cities, African Americans are serving longer prison sentences than White Americans.[143]

❰

Martin Luther King, Jr. hoped that one day his children would be judged by the "content of their character and not by the color of their skin." He foresaw a time when "the sons of former slaves and the sons of former slave owners would be able to sit down together at the table of brotherhood." Unfortunately, 30 years after King's death, on college campuses across the nation, Black and White students are voluntarily segregating themselves. The inevitable results include tensions, misunderstandings and on occasion violence. *U. S. News and World Report* conducted a survey of race relations on college campuses in 1993. The magazine interviewed 550 student editors and discovered:

- 49% of the respondents described race relations on campus as poor;
- 37% said that Blacks on their campus feel that "Whites are hostile and aloof";
- 24% felt that White students were physically afraid of Blacks;

- 71% reported that during the past year there had been at least one incident on campus that could be considered racial.[144]

Clearly racism persists on the campuses of our institutions of higher learning.

Since President Harry Truman integrated the Armed Forces in 1948, the military has been viewed as a leader in racial equality. It has been cited as a model of successful Affirmative Action. In 1999 *The Washington Post* reported the results of a Congressional survey of racial attitudes in the military. The survey revealed that 75% of all active duty African Americans and other minorities interviewed felt they had experienced racially offensive behavior. Less than 50% believed that complaints of racism are thoroughly investigated. Other complaints included the belief that Blacks and other minorities had received inferior assignments and evaluations due to race. Nevertheless, most interviewees felt that the situation in the military was better than in the civilian world. White servicemen interviewed had sharply differing observations.[145] Racism continues to permeate and infect the daily lives of Black Americans within an institution that, for more than 45 years, has been considered a model of racial equality.

Racism, institutional and individual, remains a serious American problem. It has survived attacks by legislation. It has survived decisions of the courts. Whenever the nation begins to feel that race relations have made a turn for the better, racism will remind us that, while it is sometimes dormant, it remains a powerful force for hate. In 1998, on a June night in Texas, John King, Lawrence Brewer, and Shawn Berry finished drinking at their home and went for a drive. James Byrd was walking home from a party when the three men offered him a ride. Byrd should not have accepted the offer. Brewer and King were white supremacists who had joined the Confederate Knights of America while in prison.

After stopping at a convenience store, King drove to a secluded area where the three men beat Byrd. They then chained Byrd by his ankles to the back of Berry's truck and drove away. Byrd was still alive as he was dragged behind the truck. The following morning Byrd's decapitated body was found alongside the road. John King and Lawrence Brewer were convicted of the murder of James Byrd and sentenced to death. Shawn Berry was also convicted and sentenced to life in prison without the possibility of parole for 40 years.[146] The punishment of the three men could not restore the life of James Byrd. For African Americans the Byrd incident reaffirmed the danger of being Black in America.

(

Racism is an old problem. New problems are emerging, one of which is generational. In the late 1950s and throughout the 1960s, White parents struggled with their rebellious youngsters. For many of those parents, rock and roll music symbolized their worst fears. In the 1990s, hip-hop music is symbolic of a generation gap in the Black community. Hip-hop, as expressed in the music of Tupac Shakur and others, is not just music to the younger generation; it is a culture. It's how they talk, walk, dress, and meet the challenge of everyday existence.[147] Craig Bussey of Inglewood, California, pinpoints the generation gap when he says his parents "feel like to be somebody you had to be like White people. And that's not real. My generation is standing up for ours."[148] Elinor Tatum is being groomed by her father to succeed him at the *Amsterdam News* in Harlem. She expresses it somewhat differently. She says that the difference between her generation and her father's "is that then they had hope."[149]

Bussey and Tatum know of the successes of the civil rights movement, but they are also speaking to the fact that those gains have not been sustained. Integration was supposed to bring equality. As successful Blacks have moved into formerly all White areas, integration has brought increased poverty and an absence of positive role models to the inner cities. Affirmative Action was supposed to bring economic opportunity, yet by 1988, one in four Black children "lived below *half* the poverty level."[150] It has also brought resentment among Whites, division among Blacks, and by 1999, a movement to eliminate it altogether. Although the hip-hop generation is no longer prevented from sitting at a lunch counter or sharing a bus terminal waiting room, it encounters a different kind of racism. Shauntae Brown, 26, a University of Kansas graduate student, explains: "For us it's more subtle: being followed in a store or not being able to get a cab."[151] It doesn't matter if people are highly successful or underprivileged, if they are Black they will be treated as a suspect.

The older generations looked to Martin Luther King, Jr., Malcolm X, and Jesse Jackson for leadership. The hip-hop generation has embraced Louis Farrakhan. His message that being Black is noble, something of which to be proud, resonates within the hip-hop generation. Jason Broom of Kansas City, Missouri, says: "I love Farrakhan without question or reservation. He's a strong stand-up Black man. I don't practice his religion, but I support him. He never turned on us on the street. He's for turning us into men."[152]

The hip-hop culture's focus on pride in being Black has had mixed results. It is expressed in the inner cities and the suburbs in the music, dress, and attitudes of the younger generation. It is partially a rejection of things White. As such, it has had an unfortunately negative effect in schools. Students excelling in their work are somehow perceived to be too White by their peers.[153] Parents have faced the dilemma of encouraging their children to study only to be rebuffed. Acceptance by one's peers is a powerful motivation. If acceptance requires one to do poorly in school, it is tragic.

As was the case with rock and roll, the older generations, Black and White, judge the hip-hop generation by stereotype. Their judgments are often based on fear and misunderstanding. However, the violence and despair portrayed by Hollywood, MTV, and the media does not accurately describe the hip-hop generation as a whole. A 1997 article in *Newsweek* described Antwan Allen as sixteen years old, an orphan living with his aunt in Harlem, and attending La Salle Academy. He was number-one in his class, president of the drama club, president of the student council, editor of the school newspaper, and president of the honor society. He hoped to attend Cornell University or the University of Pennsylvania and planned for a career in public service.[154] Antwan contends: "Not all Black people speak in slang, wear jeans hanging off them and are getting high. That's what's portrayed on TV." He says: "I can keep it real on the street corner with my homies, but where is that going to get me in life. Is it going to get me a good job? Is it going to get me a good family?" Nevertheless, Antwan is not out of touch with hip-hopsters. He admired Tupac Shakur when the singer's music talked of the positive roles of single mothers. When Shakur focused on cop killings and *gangsta rap* Antwan was turned off.[155]

Antwan Allen is a unique individual, but he is not alone among his generation to reject the "street-thug" stereotype. One example is the Harlem Boys Choir. Countless other examples of children striving to better themselves can be found in any inner city Boys and Girls Club. Unfortunately, for most of America they are invisible.[156]

On June 13, 1997, President Clinton's Executive Order 13050 created the Initiative on Race and established an Advisory Board to advise the President on how to build *One America for the 21st Century*.[157] The Advisory Board was charged with the following mission:

> The Advisory Board shall advise the President on matters involving race and racial conciliation, including ways in which the President can:
>
> 1. Promote constructive national dialogue to confront and work through challenging issues that surround race;
>
> 2. Increase the nation's understanding of our recent history of race relations and the course our Nation is charting on issues of race relations and racial diversity;
>
> 3. Bridge racial divides by encouraging leaders in communities throughout the Nation to develop and implement innovative approaches to calming racial tensions;
>
> 4. Identify, develop, and implement solutions to problems in areas in which race has a substantial impact, such as education, economic opportunity, housing, health care, and the administration of justice.[158]

Fifteen months later, after meeting, talking, and listening to Americans of all races, economic status, religious beliefs, and political persuasions, the Advisory Board issued its report.

It is not surprising that the Advisory Board concluded that there is in fact a gap between the experiences and opportunities of White Americans as opposed to the experiences and opportunities of Black Americans and other minorities. It found that, notwithstanding the achievements of the Civil Rights Movement, barriers remain that prevent people of color from being fully included in American society. These barriers include active discrimination in employment, pay, and housing.[159] When one considers existing legislation governing equal opportunity in employment and the Federal Fair Housing Acts, the conclusions of the Advisory Board on these matters are shocking. They confirm the hold that racism has on White America and the magnitude of the problem to be solved.

Racism in America is the legacy of the slave system. Slaves provided a cheap, reliable labor force, but ownership of human beings is not a natural circumstance. Therefore, to make the practice palatable it was necessary to convince the public that slaves were an inferior race suited for bondage. The slave owners cultivated this theory so effectively that, more than 400 years later, it remains in the American conscience. Myths have developed that, although untrue, are accepted by the White community as fact. Today, inferiority is more often expressed in terms of lack of ambition and laziness. African Americans are viewed as more prone to violence and crime. They are accused of being unwilling to accept responsibility and prone to blame others for their problems. Surveys taken in 1977 and again in 1997 showed that the majority of Whites believed that "the main reason Blacks tend to have worse jobs, income, and housing than Whites is that they just don't have the motivation or the will power to pull themselves up out of poverty."[160]

Overt racism, myth, or simple misunderstandings are the linchpins of the gap between the races in America. Although there is much to be accomplished in employment, economic opportunity, and fair housing, the Advisory Board focused on youth as the greatest hope for bridging the racial divide.[161] It will be in the schools where change will occur. Integrated schools where students must interact with diverse races are the vehicle for changing attitudes. The curriculum, however, must provide the basis for understanding. Schools can no longer offer a strictly Eurocentric version of world history. American history courses must reflect an accurate account of the African American experience. Of equal importance teachers, Black and White, must be trained not only in the contents of the new curriculum, but also how to teach it. Eliminating racism and bridging the racial divide cannot wait for a new generation to mature.

(

The face of America is changing. While White Americans constitute 73% of the population in 1999, by 2050 the United States will be approximately 53% White, 25% Hispanic, 12% Black, 8% Asian Pacific American, and 1% American Indian and Alaskan Natives.[162] The reality of these projected demographics requires a change in racial attitudes and perceptions. The question is, can it be done? In a 1998 interview Martin Luther King, III, said that if he could have a conversation with his father today, the first question he would ask would be: "Where did we go wrong?"[163] We don't know what his father would say, but perhaps the answer would be that we haven't taken the next step. The focus of the civil rights effort of Martin Luther King, Jr.'s time was on integration, on eliminating Jim Crow laws, desegregating schools, and removing a myriad of formal barriers that separated the races. Integration, however, did not change entrenched attitudes, dispel myths, or create understanding between cultures with sometimes vastly different traditions. Those are the things that must now be changed.

After the tragic events from the Rodney King incident, Ron Smith and Dave Johnson, two ministers in St. Paul, Minnesota, began a series of personal discussions on the racial divide. Their talks forced them to take a good look at themselves. Johnson came to realize how much he had benefited by simply being White. He calls it *White privilege*. Smith wrestled with his fear of being betrayed by a White man.[164] When they began their talks in May 1992, the Reverend Smith was pastor of the Open Door Baptist Church. His congregation was entirely Black. The Reverend Johnson was pastor of the Park Baptist Church. His congregation was entirely White. By 1999, the two ministers merged their churches and now serve as co-pastors of the Unity Baptist Church.

Smith and Johnson call the process they used to merge their churches Racial Reconciliation. "In Racial Reconciliation, individuals consciously strive to overcome the legacy of racism, first by forging genuine bonds with at least one person of a different race."[165] The two ministers met two or three times a week over coffee and simply talked about matters in general. As time passed they ventured into more personal subjects. They prayed together and eventually were able to openly discuss their feelings about race and explore the rationale behind their attitudes. In time, each was able to recognize where change was needed in his personal life.

From this beginning they took the first steps in bringing their congregations together. Smith preached at Park Baptist, Johnson at Open Door Baptist. In August 1993, the parishioners attended each other's parishes. Eventually, they met as a group and talked. At this point there was still no plan to merge the churches. In fact, the two congregations referred to any talk of merger as the "M" word.[166] By late 1994, the two congregations agreed to worship together each Sunday for a period of four months.

Worshiping together each week for an extended time proved to be an enlightening experiment. Differences soon surfaced. How long should the service last? What songs should be sung? Should the congregation listen quietly to the sermon or respond vocally? Many Whites objected to the Blacks' worship style. Blacks, in turn, felt restrained. Whites were uncomfortable. For the first time they were in a group where they were not the majority. Blacks were giving up something very precious.

Church was the one place they could be entirely with people of their own race. It was a place they could be themselves. Nevertheless, in February 1998, despite the differences, the two churches voted to merge and became the Unity Baptist Church.

In 1992, two congregations, one Black and one White, worshiped in isolation. They shared the same belief in God, yet they were strangers. Through the process of Racial Reconciliation they were able to overcome their misunderstandings, fears, and jealousies and bond together in brotherhood. Hopefully, the seeds of Racial Reconciliation will find fertile soil in twenty-first century America.

NOTES

91. Ralph David Abernathy. *And When The Walls Came Tumbling Down* (New York: Harper and Row, 1989) pp. 448-449

92. Abernathy p. 450

93. Abernathy p. 400

94. Abernathy p. 404

95. Abernathy p. 409

96. Abernathy pp. 409-410

97. L. Mpho Mabunda, ed. *The African Almanac* (7th edition) Gale Research, Detroit, 1997, p. 438

98. African Almanac p. 588

99. Bennett p. 579

100. Jay P. Pederson, ed. and Jesse Carney Smith, ed. *African American Breakthroughs* (New York: Gale Research, Inc., 1995) p. 178

101. Bennett p. 433

102. African American Breakthroughs p. 160

103. Encyclopedia of Black America pp. 357-359

104. Encyclopedia of Black America pp. 341-342

105. Casey Seller, "A history of intolerance belies Vermont's neighborly self-image," *Burlington Free Press* (April 25,1999) p. 9A

106. Encyclopedia of Black America p. 337

107. Lisa Cozzens, " Boston Under the Phase I Plan," *School Integration 1955-1975, African American History* (25May1998). Internet 27 January 2000 http://www.watson.org/~lisa/blackhistory/school-integration/boston/ phaseI.html

108. Lisa Cozzens, "Phase II In Action," School Integration 1955-1975, African American History (25 May 1998). Internet 27 January 2000. http://www. watson.org/~lisa/blackhistory/school-integration/bosto/actII.html

109. Bill Delaney, "On Boston,busing and walking to school," *CNN.com* (18 March 1999). Internet 29 January 2000. http://www9.cnn.com/SPECIALS/views/y/ 1999/03/delaney.busing.mar18/

110. Darrell Pressley, "Mayor: New schools would dismantle busing in Boston." The Boston Herald.Com (14 January 1999). Internet 29 January 2000. http://www. bostonherald.com/bostonherald/lonw/sku101141999htm

111. Delaney. p. 3

112. Beth Daley, "Boston school busing fading as a key issue." *The Boston Globe* (19 January 1999). Internet 29 January 2000 http://charlotte.com/2000/docs/0120 boston.htm

113. Bennett p. 436

114. Bennett p. 437

115. Owen M. Fiss, "Affirmative Action: Beyond Diversity," Washington Post.com (7 May 1997).p.A21.Internet 8 February 2000. http://www.washingtonpost.com /wp-srv/politics/special/affirm/stories/aaop050797.htm

116. George Stephanopoulos and Christopher Edley, Jr. Affirmative Action Review "Report to the President." *AFFIRMATIVE ACTION:HISTORY AND RATIONALE.* (19 July 1995) p. 4. Internet 5 February 2000. http://www.white house.gov/ WH/EOP/OP/html/aa/aa02.html

117. Stephanopoulos and Edley p. 4.

118. Stephanopoulos and Edley p. 5

119. Louis Freedberg, "After 20 Years, Bakke Ruling Back in the Spotlight." *San Francisco Chronicle.* (Chronicle Sections, Saturday June 28, 1998). p. 2-3

120. "RACE AND GENDER IN AMERICA," *Californians Against Discrimination and Preferences(CADAP).* (26 April 1998). Internet 14 June 2000. http://www.cadap. org/

121. "History of CADAP" Role as Defendant-Interventor in Coalition for Economic Equity v. Pete Wilson (Federal Lawsuit Addressing the Constitutionality of Prop. 209)" *Californians Against Discrimination and Preferences.* Internet. 7 February 2000. http://www.cadap.org/timeline.html

122. Sue Anne Pressley, "Texas Campus Attracts Fewer Minorities." Washingtonpost. com (28 August 1997). Internet 8 February 2000. http://www.washington post.com/wp-srv/politics/special/affirm/stories/ aa082897.htm

123. Pressley p. 1

124. Kenneth J. Cooper, "Affirmative Action Challenged." *The Boston Sunday Globe* (December 26,1999) p. A22

125. Dimitri B.Papadimitriou, Employment Policy, Community Development, and the Underclass. *The Jerome Levy Economics Institute* (Feb. 10, 1998). p. 1. Internet 3 March 2000 http://netec.ier.hit.u.ac.jp/WoPEc/data/Papers/wpawwuwpma 9802016.html

126. Papadimitriou p. 1

127. Jacob V. Lamar, Jr. "Today's Native Sons," *Time* December 1, 1986 pp. 26-27

128. Richard Lacayo, "Between Two World," *Time* Vol. 133 No.11 (March 13, 1989) p. 62.

129. Ellis Close, "The Good News About Black America," *U.S. News & World Report* (June 7, 1999), pp. 30-31

130. Close, p. 40

131. Willam A. Henry III, "Pride and Prejudice." *Time* Vol. 143 No.9 (February 28, 1994), pp. 21-22

132. Henry III, pp. 21-27

133. L. Mpho Mabunda, ed. *The African American Almanac* (7th Edition), Gale Research. Detroit 1997. p. 599

134. David A. Harris, "Driving While Black." *An American Civil Liberties Union Special Report.* June 1999. p. 2. Internet 20 February 2000 http://www. aclu.org/profiling/ report/index.html

135. Harris p. 6

136. Harris p. 5

137. Harris p. 8

138. Harris p. 10

139. Harris p. 11

140. Harris p. 12

141. Harris p. 12

142. "Crack Cocaine Sentencing Policy: Unjustified and Unreasonable," *The Sentencing Project* (Briefing/Facts Sheets) p. 1, Internet 21 March 2000. http://www.sentenc-ingproject.org/brief/1003.htm

143. The Sentencing Project p. 2

144. Mel Elfin, "RACE On Campus" *U.S. News and World Report* (April 19, 1993), p. 53

145. Robert Suro, and Michael A. Fletcher, "75 Percent Of Military's Minorities See Racism," *The Washington Post* (Nov. 23, 1999), p. A1

146. Bryan Robinson, "Third dragging defendant avoids death penalty, gets life sentence," Court TV on Line (Nov. 18,1999), pp. 1-4, Internet 25 February 2000. http://www.courttv.com/trials/berry/111899 sentence ctv.htm

147. John Leland, and Allison Samuels, "The New Generation Gap," *Newsweek* (March 17, 1997) p. 54

148. Leland p. 54

149. Leland p. 56

150. Leland p. 56

151. Leland p. 57

152. Leland p. 57

153. Kate Zernike, "Talking about the black - white gap" *The Boston Sunday Globe* (October 31,1999). p. E2

154. Ellis Close, "The Black Gen X Nobody Knows," *Newsweek* (March 17,1997). p. 62

155. Close p. 62

156. Close p. 62

157. "Executive Summary". *One America in the 21st Century: Forging A New Future.* (18 September 1998) p. 1. Internet 27 March 2000. http://www.whitehouse.gov/Initiatives/OneAmerica/PIR_summary.pdf

158. Clinton, William,J. "PRESIDENT'S ADIVSORY BOARD ON RACE *Executive Order 13050.*" June 13, 1997. p. 1. Internet 2 February 2000 http://www.pub.whitehouse.gov/uri-res/12R?urn:pdi://oma.eop.gov.us/1997/6/13/9.text.2

159. One America in the 21st Century, p. 4

160. Jesse Thornton and David Whitman, "Whites' myths about blacks," *U.S. News and World Report* (November 9, 1992). pp. 41-44

161. One America in the 21st Century, p. 8

162. One America in the 21st Century, p. 3

163. "Martin Luther King III: Can He Step Forward?" *The Burlington Free Press: USA WEEKEND* (January 16-18, 1998) p. 4

164. Frank Clancy, "How one small church bridges the RACIAL DIVIDE," *The Burlington Free Press: USA WEEKEND* (September 10-12,1999) p. 6

165. Clancy, p. 7

166. Clancy, p. 7

INDEX

SOURCES

"A history of intolerance belies Vermont's neighborly self-image," *Burlington Free Press* (April 25,1999), p. 9A.

Abernathy, Ralph, David. *And When The Walls Came Tumbling Down.* New York: Harper and Row, 1989.

"Affirmative Action." *CQ Researcher* 1991, p 286.

"Affirmative Action Challenged." *The Boston Sunday Globe* (December 26,1999), p A22.

Andrews, William. *Six Women's Slave Narratives.* New York: Oxford University Press, 1988.

"Beckwith Trial Stirs Mississippi Ghosts," *Boston Sunday Globe* (January 16, 1994),p 1.

Bennett Jr. Lerone. *Before The Mayflower; A History of Black America.* New York: Penguin, 1987.

Bentley, Judith. *Harriet Tubman.* New York; Franklin Watts, 1990.

Bishop, Jim. *The Days Of Martin Luther King, Jr.* New York: G.P. Putnam & Sons, 1971.

Blaustein, Albert and Zangrando, Robert. *Civil Rights and the Black American: A Documentary History.* New York: Washington Square Press, 1968.

"Black woman chosen to lead Smith College." *Boston Globe* (December 16,1994) p 38.

Boorstin, Daniel and Kelley, Brooks. *A History of the United States Since 1861.* New Jersey: Prentice Hall, 1989.

Clancy, Frank. "How one small church bridges the racial divide," *The Burlington Free Press: USA Weekend* (September 10-12,1999) p 6.

Clark, Leon E., ed. *The African Past And Coming of the European.* New York: Praeger Publishers, 1970.

Clinton, William J. "President's Advisory Board on Race, Executive Order 13050." June 13, 1997, p 1. Internet 2 February 2000 http://www.pub.whitehouse. gov/uri-res/12R?urn:pdi://oma.eop.gov.us/1997/6/13/9.text.2.

Close, Ellis. "The Good News About Black America," *U.S. News & World Report* (June 7,1999), pp 30-31.

Close, Ellis. "The Black Gen X Nobody Knows," *Newsweek* (March 17,1997) p 62.

Cozzens, Lisa. "Boston Under the Phase I Plan," *School Integration 1955-1975,African American History* (25May1998). Internet 27 January 2000, http://www.watson.org/~lisa/blackhistory/school-integration/boston/phaseI.html.

Cozzens,Lisa. "Phase II In Action, *School Integration 1955-1975,African American History* (25 May 1998). Internet 27 January 2000. http://www.watson.org/~lisa/blackhistory/school-integration/bosto/actII.html.

"Crack Cocaine Sentencing Policy: Unjustified and Unreasonable," *The Sentencing Project* (Briefing/Facts Sheets) p 1, Internet 21 March 2000. http://www.sentencingproject. org/brief/1003.htm.

Daley,Beth. "Boston school busing fading as a key issue," *The Boston Globe* (19 January 1999). Internet 29 January 2000, http://charlotte.com/2000/docs/0120boston.htm.

David, Jay. *Growing Up Black.* New York: William Morrow & Company, 1969.

Delaney, Bill. "On Boston,busing and walking to schoo," *CNN.com* (18 March 1999). Internet 29 January 2000. http://www9.cnn.com/SPECIALS/views/y/1999/03/delaney.busing.mar18/.

De Las Casas, Bartolome, *The Devastation of the Indies.* Baltimore: The Johns Hopkins University Press, 1974.

Elfin, Mel. "Race on Campus," *U.S. News and World Report* (April 19, 1993), p.53.

"Executive Summary." *One America in the 21st Century: Forging A New Future.* (18 September 1998) p. 1. Internet 27 March 2000. http://www.whitehouse.gov/Initiatives/OneAmerica/PIR_summary.pdf.

Fiss, Owen, M. "Affirmative Action: Beyond Diversity", Washington Post.com (7 May 1997).p.A21.Internet 8 February 2000. http://www.washingtonpost.com/wp-srv/politics/special/affirm/stories/aaop050797.htm

Forman, Robert. Black Ghettos, White Ghettos, And Slums. New Jersey: Prentice Hall, 1971.

Franklin, John Hope and Starr Isidore. *The Negro In Twentieth Century America.* New York: Vintage Books, 1967.

Franklin, John Hope, ed. *Three Negro Classics; Up From Slavery, The Souls of Black Folk, The Autobiography of an Ex-Colored Man.* New York: Avon, 1965.

Freedberg, Louis. "After 20 Years, Bakke Ruling Back in the Spotlight." *San Francisco Chronicle.* (Chronicle Sections, Saturday June 28, 1998). p. 2-3.

Ginzberg, Eli and Eichner, Alfred. *The Troublesome Presence; American Democracy and the Negro.* New York: The Free Press of Glencoe, 1964.

Glines, C. V. "The Red-Tailed Fighters." *The Retired Officer Magazine,* Volume XLVIII No.9 (September 1992), p. 26.

"Glory." Burbank, California: RCA/Columbia Pictures Home Video, 1990

Grant, Joanne. *Black Protest; History, Documents and Analyses 1619 to the Present.* Greenwich: Fawcett, 1968.

Gregory, Dick. *Write Me In.* New York: Bantam, 1968.

Griffin, John. *Black Like Me.* New York: Penguin, 1960.

Hamilton, Charles V. *Adam Clayton Powell, Jr.* New York: Atheneum, 1991.

Hampton, Henry, executive producer, Judith Vecchione, series senior producer. *Eyes on the Prize.* , Boston, Massachusetts: Blackside Inc., Premiere airdate: January 1987.

Harlan, Louis, R. *Booker T. Washington The Wizard Of Tuskegee, 1901-1915.* New York: Oxford University Press, 1983.

Harris, David A. "Driving While Black". *An AmericanCivil Liberties Union Special Report.* June 1999. p.2. Internet 20 February 2000, http://www. aclu.org/profiling/report/index.html

Haskins, James . *The Scottsboro Boys.* New York: Henry Holt and Company, 1994.

Henry III, William A. "Pride and Prejudice." *Time* Vol. 143 No.9 (February 28,1994) p. 21-27.

Herskovits, Melvin. *The Myth of the Negro Past.* Boston: Beacon, 1941.

"History of CADAP's Role as Defendant-Interventor in Coalition for Economic Equity v. Pete Wilson (Federal Lawsuit Addressing the Constitutionality of Prop. 209)" *Californians Against Discrimination and Preferences.* Internet. 7 February 2000. http://www.cadap.org/timeline.html

"House Divided." Miami, Florida: WPBT, 1982.

Hughes, Langston. *The Ways of White Folks.* New York: Random House, 1934.

Hughes, Langston; Meltzer, Milton; and Lincoln, Eric. *A Pictorial History of Black Americans.* New York: Crown, 1956.

"Jackie Robinson," *The Lincoln Library of Sports Champions,* 1974, Vol.11, 20-27

"Joe Louis," *The Lincoln Library of Sports Champions,* 1974, Vol.8, 54-61.

Hauser, Thomas. *Muhammad Ali; His Life and Times.* New York: Simon & Schuster, 1991.

Killens, John. *Black Man's Burden.* New York: Pocket Books, 1969.

"King: Montgomery to Memphis." Beverly Hills California: Pacific Arts Video, 1988.

Kluger, Richard. *Simple Justice.* New York: Alfred A. Knopf, 1976.

Lacayo, Richard. " Between Two Worlds." *Time,* Vol.133 No.11 (March 13, 1989), p. 62.

Lamar, Jacob V., Jr. "Today's Native Sons," *Time,* December 1, 1986 pp. 26-27.

Lacayo,Richard. "Between Two Worlds," *Time,* Vol.133 No.11, (March 13, 1989), p.62.

Leland, John and Samuels, Allison. "The New Generation Gap." *Newsweek* (March 17,1997). p. 54.

Leland, John and Smith, Vern E. "Echoes of Little Rock." Newsweek, (September 29, 1997) p.52.

Lewis, David Levering. *W.E.B. Du Bois: Biography of a Race.* New York: Henry Holt and Company, 1993

Low, W. Augustus and Clift, Virgil A., eds. *Encyclopedia of Black America.* New York: McGraw-Hill Inc., 1981.

Lubell, Samuel. *White & Black.* New York: Harper & Row, 1966.

Mabunda, L. Mpho, ed. *The African Almanac.* Detroit: Gale, 1997

Marine, Gene. *The Black Panthers.* New York: Signet, 1969.

"Martin Luther King III: Can He Step Forward?" *The Burlington Free Press: USA Today* (January 16-18, 1998) p. 4.

Mead, Chris. "Black Hero In A White Land." *Sports Illustrated* (March 16,1985), p. 81.

Muhammed Ali. New York, New York: HBO VIDEO, 1989.

Oates, Stephen B. *Let the Trumpet Sound.* New York: Harpers & Row Publishers 1982.

Papadimitriou, Dimitri B. "Employment Policy, Community Develpoment, and the Underclass." *The Jerome Levy Economics Institute* (Feb. 10, 1998).p.1. Internet 3 March 2000. http://netec.ier.hit-u.ac.jp/WoPEc/data/Papers/wpawuwpma9802016. html

Parks, Rosa. *My Story.* New York: Dial Books, 1992.

Pederson, Jay, P. and Jesse Carney Smith, Jesse Carney, eds. *African American Breakthroughs.* New York: Gale Research, Inc., 1995

Perry, Marvin; Scholl, Allan; Davis, Daniel; Harris, Jeannette, and Von Laue, Theodore. *History of the World.* Atlanta: Houghton Mifflin, 1990.

Powell, Colin. *My American Journey.* New York: Random House, 1995.

Pressley, Darrell. "Mayor: New schools would dismantle busing in Boston." The Boston Herald.Com (14 January 1999). Internet 29 January 2000. http://www.bostonherald. com/bostonherald/lonw/sku101141999.htm

Pressley, Sue Anne. "Texas Campus Attracts Fewer Minorities." Washingtonpost.com (28 August 1997). Internet 8 February 2000. http://www.washingtonpost.com/wp-srv/politics/special/affirm/stories/aa082897.htm

"RACE AND GENDER IN AMERICA" *Californians Against Discrimination and Preferences(CADAP).* (26 April 1998). Internet 14 June 2000. http://www.cadap.org/

"Racial Quota." *The CQ Researcher 1991,* 279-285.

Robinson, Bryan. "Third dragging defendant avoids death penalty, gets life sentence," "Court TV on Line" (Nov. 18,1999), pp.1-4, Internet 25 February 2000. http://www.courttv.com/trials'berry/111899_sentence_ctv.htm

Rowan, Carl. *Dream Makers, Dream Breakers; The World of Justice Thurgood Marshall.* Boston: Little Brown and Company, 1993.

"75 Percent of Military's Minorities See Racism," *The Washington Post* (Nov. 23, 1999), p A1 & A10.

Stephanopoulos, George and Edley, Christopher, Jr. "Affirmative Action Review: Report to the President." *Affirmative Action: History and Rationale* (19 July 1995) p.4.Internet 5 February 2000. http://www.whitehouse.gov/WH/EOP/OP/ html/aa/aa02.html

"Talking about the black-white gap." *The Boston Sunday Globe* (October 31, 1999). p E2

"The Four Girls." *The Boston Globe Magazine,* (February 3, 1991), p 15

"The Search For Black Identity: Malcolm X." Pleasantville, New York: Guidance Associates Sound Filmstrips, 1970

"The Search for Black Identity: Proud Heritage from Africa" (Part 1): Pleasantville, New York: Guidance Associates Sound Filmstrips, 1970

Thornton, Jesse and Whitman, David. "Whites' myths about blacks." *U.S. News and World Report* (November 9, 1992). pp. 41-44

Todd, Lewis Paul and Curti, Merle. *Rise of the American Nation,* Vol. 1. New York: Harcourt Brace Jovanovich Publishers, 1982

Tyack, David. *Nobody Knows: Black Americans in the Twentieth Century.* London: The Macmillan Company, 1969

U. S. Army Forces Command. *Black Americans: A Military Perspective.* Fort McPherson, GA, January 1983

Vezina, Merideth R. "In Limbo at Lockett." *The Retired Officer Magazine,* Volume L, No. 2 (February 1994) p 28

Wade, Richard. *Negroes in American Life.* Boston: Houghton Mifflin, 1965

Washington, Booker T. *Up from Slavery.* Williamstown: Corner House Publishers, 1971

Watters, Pat. *Down to Now: Reflections on the Southern Civil Rights Movement.* NewYork: Random House, 1971

Witherspoon, Wm. Roger. *Martin Luther King, Jr.: To the Mountaintop.* New York: Doubleday & Company Inc., 1985

X, Malcolm. *The Autobiography of Malcolm X.* New York: Grove Press, Inc., 1964

The Authors

ROBERT L. WALSH was raised in Swampscott, Massachusetts. He received his bachelor of arts degree from Colgate University in 1955 and his masters degree in education from the University of Vermont in 1979. He taught African American history at South Burlington High School, South Burlington, Vermont from 1980-1995. Prior to entering the teaching profession, Mr. Walsh completed a career in the United States Marine Corps, retiring with the rank of Lieutenant Colonel. He served as a member of the Vermont House of Representatives from 1983-1989. Mr. Walsh is currently a member of the adjunct faculty at the University of Vermont and resides in South Burlington, Vermont.

LEON F. BURRELL was raised in Port Huron, Michigan. He received his doctorate of philosophy in higher education administration from Michigan State University and his post-doctorate in school social work from the University of McGill. He is now an emeritus professor of the College of Education and Social Services at the University of Vermont. During his twenty-five years at the university he developed and taught courses in Higher Education, Social Work and Cultural Diversity. He has published three books and numerous articles on matters relating to research on minority students in higher education, alcoholism in the family and on college campuses, and in the practice of school social work. A veteran of four years active service in the United States Air Force, and three years service in the Michigan Army National Guard, he currently resides in Burlington, Vermont.

www.ingramcontent.com/pod-product-compliance
Lightning Source LLC
Chambersburg PA
CBHW071337280526
45787CB00001B/127